MW00786056

TABLE OF CONTENTS

Top 20 Test Taking Tips

1. Carefully follow all the test registration procedures
2. Know the test directions, duration, topics, question types, how many questions
3. Setup a flexible study schedule at least 3-4 weeks before test day
4. Study during the time of day you are most alert, relaxed, and stress free
5. Maximize your learning style; visual learner use visual study aids, auditory learner use auditory study aids
6. Focus on your weakest knowledge base
7. Find a study partner to review with and help clarify questions
8. Practice, practice, practice
9. Get a good night's sleep; don't try to cram the night before the test
10. Eat a well balanced meal
11. Know the exact physical location of the testing site; drive the route to the site prior to test day
12. Bring a set of ear plugs; the testing center could be noisy
13. Wear comfortable, loose fitting, layered clothing to the testing center; prepare for it to be either cold or hot during the test
14. Bring at least 2 current forms of ID to the testing center
15. Arrive to the test early; be prepared to wait and be patient
16. Eliminate the obviously wrong answer choices, then guess the first remaining choice
17. Pace yourself; don't rush, but keep working and move on if you get stuck
18. Maintain a positive attitude even if the test is going poorly
19. Keep your first answer unless you are positive it is wrong
20. Check your work, don't make a careless mistake

Fundamentals of Technology Education

Career and technical education course approval and re-approval process

According to the Carl D. Perkins Career and Technical Education Improvement Act of 2006, career and technical education (CTE) programs in all states must emulate the New York CTE program. In Washington, the CTE program has the following goals:

- Maintaining rigorous academic standards.
- Providing the skills necessary to fill any deficiencies or gaps in Washington's economy.
- Ensuring that all state education reform requirements are aligned.
- Creating and designing good career and technical education programs by building and facilitating relationships with local CTE advisory councils.

The approval/re-approval process for CTE courses can be performed online. Approval requests are due April 15 for first-semester courses and October 15 for the second-semester courses. Additionally, re-approval requests for programs must be received by January 31. Approval and re-approval for specific courses follow a schedule that can found at the same site.

Safety and health standards

The Safety Guide for Career and Technical Education contains the most recent instructions and checklists for vocational education curricula. This lengthy document is published by OSPI, and can be found online. It contains a comprehensive list of safety practices and requirements that students and teachers should observe in CTE courses. These practices and requirements include the following:

- Proper floor cleanliness and maintenance.
- Proper maintenance, storage, and handling of power tools, shop machinery, and equipment.
- Required shop equipment.
- Safety rules and standards displayed in plain sight.
- Proper material handling and storage.
- Storage, labeling, and handling of electrical devices and equipment.
- Disposal of hazardous waste.
- Non-asbestos fire blankets.
- Proper safety equipment, such as eyewear and face shields.
- Eye wash stations.
- Proper ventilation.
- Safety Signs.
- Ambient noise level limits.

Career and technical education curriculum advisory committee

The career and technical education (CTE) advisory committee is responsible for determining and recommending a curriculum that will best prepare students for passing state assessments and earning a Certificate of Academic Achievement, or CAA. The specific duties of the CTE advisory committee include the following:

- Establishing criteria, processes, and tools that state and district boards will use to identify and evaluate appropriate CTE equivalency courses. These courses should gain equivalent academic credit in the core subject areas of math, science, social studies, English, health/fitness, and art.
- Using these criteria, processes, and tools to determine if existing

CTE courses fulfill the equivalency requirements.

Tech Prep articulation

Tech Prep is a high school program that provides students with technical training, applied academics, and assistance in finding workplace internship and guidance. Tech Prep offers a number of advantages to high school students:

- Provides college credit, ultimately saving both time and money. Tech Prep enables high school graduates to bypass entry level courses and enroll in higher level classes. The manner in which college credit and standing are awarded is based on an articulation agreement between the high school and the college program. In most cases, this agreement awards college credit using tests, certification by a high school teacher, or college course completion.
- Prepares high school students for the rigors of college courses.
- Prepares high school students for a career in technical professions, such as engineering, science, health care, computers, etc. Upon leaving college, tech Prep students often receive better wages and benefits than students who did not take Tech Prep courses.

Membership in professional career and technical organizations

There are many different professional career and technical organizations. When deciding which organization to join, the best choice will vary depending on the specific CTE field and personal preference. However, most organizations offer similar benefits, such as the following:

- Networking and professional development opportunities through expos, seminars, and webinars. Members have the opportunity to meet and speak with CTE educators, business partners, institutional representatives, and policy makers.
- Helpful classroom tools, best practices, and analysis.
- Partnerships with and access to industry experts.
- A news periodical that keeps members up-to-date on the newest developments in the field.
- Awards programs that offer national recognition.
- Online courses that may improve career advancement prospects.
- Job banks.
- Connection to other education worldwide.

Primary business management functions

Business management usually includes the following functions:

- Planning – involves creating plans for action based on forecasts over certain periods of time, such as weeks, months, and years.
- Organizing – requires the optimization of resource usage so that plans will be successful and can be carried out in the most efficient ways possible.
- Staffing – recruits and assigns personnel to the appropriate jobs. This function involves job analysis.
- Directing – identifies the specific tasks necessary for plan completion, and getting workers to carry them out.
- Monitoring – checks the progress of the project team against the

plan, and determines whether it is on schedule.

- Motivating – is fundamental and a very important aspect of business management. Workers must be motivated to carry out their specific tasks, and contribute to other functions.

Work schedule

A work schedule breaks a project down into its most basic work activities. These activities are known as terminal elements, and cannot be further divided into smaller tasks. The work schedule will include estimates for the resources, cost, and duration of each activity, and then arrange them by their dependencies and order of completion. To create a work schedule, the project manager must have a work breakdown structure, which includes an effort estimate and the resource availability for each task. There is software that can perform much of the work necessary to create a work schedule; however, even when using these applications, the manager must have an understanding of certain key concepts and tools, such as dependencies, resource allocation, earned value, critical paths, and Gantt charts. A Gantt chart is a bar chart that shows each terminal element, its duration, and other summary information.

Workflow tracking

A workflow is an abstraction of work that is performed by a single person or group of people. It depicts a sequence of steps that, upon completion, produces a certain outcome or product. Any workflow must have input, such as information or materials. This input then undergoes a change or transformation in accordance with certain rules. Finally, a workflow will produce an output, which consists of new information or a new product. When monitoring workflow, management may track a document as it passes through each step within the sequence. Workflow plays an important role in issue tracking, the purpose of which is identifying and resolving customer problems. A problem is input into the customer call support center (via a customer complaint), tracked as it passes through all the steps, and then resolved.

Impact of scientific and technical innovation

Scientific and technical innovation has played a major role in enhancing productivity, increasing a society's wealth, and raising its standard of living. After a new innovation comes about, it must spread to other people and groups in order to be effective. This process is known as diffusion, and is illustrated using an s-curve, also known as a diffusion curve, which tracks an increase in revenue or productivity over time. An s-curve represents the product life of an innovation. During the early stages of product life, an innovation must establish its usefulness and experiences a very slow growth in terms of revenue and productivity. The middle stages of product life see rapid increases in growth, and the latter stages of product life involve gradual decline. Product improvements may extend the lifespan of an innovation, but it will inevitably fall off. Consequently, companies are always seeking new innovations to replace older ones.

Resource management

Resource management seeks to allocate an organization's resources in the most efficient and economical ways possible—that is, the goal of resource management is the optimization of resource usage in a project. Resources include money, employees, inventory, production, and information technology, and are allocated using a variety of processes and techniques. One such technique is resource leveling, which balances usage by eliminating inventory shortages and excesses. To avoid shortages and thereby reduce conflict, management should take care when scheduling multiple activities at the same time. If concurrent activities require more of one resource than is available or make use of the same person, they should be rescheduled. In many cases, management may be forced to delay an activity until the resource becomes available. If this activity is part of the critical path, the project may be delayed.

Stimulating competitiveness and creating new goods and services

Technological innovation provides a number of benefits to the marketplace. It can introduce new products, which are simply those with which customers have no prior experience. Technological innovation can also introduce an improved or more efficient means of production or commodity handling. In many cases, these new products or means of production will open up new markets, and require the discovery of new sources of raw materials. This often stimulates the economy by creating additional competition and breaking up existing monopolies. Technological innovation is often the result of the pursuit of better quality; new market formation; new regulations; need for replacement parts or services; decreased availability of materials; increased labor costs; increased production costs; etc.

Major scientific and technological innovations

The automobile was granted a patent in 1885. Karl Benz, who is widely regarded as the inventor of the gasoline-powered car, placed the first automobiles into production during the same year.

The airplane was developed in 1903 by Wilbur and Orville Wright. They used various principles of aerodynamics, such as drag and lift, to develop the first power and controlled flight.

The integrated circuit was developed in 1958 by Jack Kilby of Texas Instruments and Robert Noyce at Fairchild Semiconductor. It led to the development of the microchip by enabling semiconductor devices to perform the same functions as vacuum tubes. It revolutionized electronic equipment, leading to the development of personal computers, cellular phones, and various digital devices.

The internet came about with the first TCP/IP protocol, which was developed in 1983 by Robert E. Kahn and Vince Cerf.

Relationship between technology and society and culture

Technology and culture have a synergistic relationship which began with the simple tools developed during the dawn of man and continues today with modern technologies such as computers and various other electronic devices. This relationship is cyclical and codependent with each party exerting influence over the other. Funding for technological development comes from two primary sources in most modern cultures and societies: Private business and enterprise, or government programs. Once new technology is developed, it influences social attitudes and beliefs, which, in turn, influence the implementation of new technology. For instance, key values and beliefs that derive from this codependence between technology and culture are the notions that human productivity should work to achieve higher levels of efficiency and that technology drives social progress. According to these beliefs, humankind is

- 8 -

improving as long as technology is improving.

Conservation and sustainability

Conservation is the effort to reduce energy and material consumption by reducing usage and making more efficient use of existing resources. New technology can facilitate conservation in a variety of ways. Renewable energy sources (geothermal, hydroelectric energy, wind power, etc.), building techniques that take advantage of the local climate, and vehicles that consume less gas (such as hybrids) all help lower energy consumption. Real-time energy metering helps consumers to better understand the impact of their energy usage.

Sustainability determines the length of time over which an ecological system will endure. Sustainable systems are those that will remain healthy and productive for a long time. Technology is often a means of increasing energy efficiency and conserving natural resources so that the human environment can become more sustainable.

Biotechnology

Biotechnology is the technological application of biology. It uses living organisms and bioprocesses to create products or processes, and has numerous applications in the following fields:
1. Medicine – includes drug production, gene therapy, gene testing, and pharmacogenomics (i.e. determining an individual's response to drugs based on inherited genetic traits).
2. Agriculture – includes enhancing crop yield, increasing nutritional attributes of food, improving crop durability, producing new substances in crop plants, and reducing dependence on agrochemicals
3. Biological engineering – uses physics, chemistry, and mathematics to solve life science problems.
4. Bioremediation and biodegradation – create organisms for purposes of removing environmental contamination.
5. Cloning –two main types: reproductive, which brings a fully developed life into the world, and therapeutic, which involves using stem cells.
6. Human Genome Project – seeks to discover all human genes, and create a reference sequence for the human genome.

Biotechnology often makes use of mathematical biology, which models complex biological processes using various types of math: graph theory, calculus, probability theory, statistics, linear algebra, abstract algebra, combinatorics, algebraic geometry, topology, dynamical systems, differential equations and coding theory.

Government regulation and facilitating technological development

Historically, the government has served a role not only in funding technological research but also in regulating its usage and side effects. One example of such regulation is the FDA, or Food and Drug administration. When selecting which types of research to fund, the government will choose those that offer the greatest benefit to mankind. However, the presence of different interest groups competing for resources can complicate the selection process. In reality, both the populace-at-large and special interests hold tremendous influence over governmental policy. The government also assumes a regulatory role in technological development, especially regarding the environment and the protection of ecological systems. The government is responsible for assigning liability to corporations whose products cause harm.

Material disposals, and environmental emission monitoring and control

Materials disposal is carried out using a variety of technologies and techniques:

- Incinerators – subject solid waste to the process of combustion in order to convert it into residue and gas. This generates heat, gas, steam, and ash.
- Landfills – eliminate solid waste by burying it.
- Recycling – reprocesses discarded materials (e.g., aluminum cans, glass bottles, newspapers, cardboard boxes, paper) into their constituent materials, and reuses them.
- Sustainability methods – include biological reprocessing, such as composting and anaerobic digestion, and energy recovery, which processes waste into fuel.

Environmental emission monitoring and control is performed by continuous emission monitoring systems, which use gas analyzers to test air samples for certain types of emissions, such as carbon dioxide, carbon monoxide, sulfur dioxide, mercury, etc. Federal programs use these systems to ensure compliance with emission standards, such as the acid rain program and other EPA standards.

Medical and agricultural technology

Medical technology includes any device, procedure, pharmaceutical, or system whose purpose is improving health, preventing sickness, and diagnosing or treating disease. Medical technology covers a vast number of healthcare products, which often make use of mathematical principles and concepts. For instance, medical imaging machines (CAT, ultrasound, etc.) and pharmacology often make use of trigonometric functions for measurement problems. Mathematical tools such as dimensional analysis are often used to calculate the correct dosage for patients.

Agricultural technology encompasses a wide array of machinery, processes, and systems designed to enhance agricultural production. Agricultural technology also makes use of mathematical principles and concepts. For instance, dimensional analyses are often used to examine complex agricultural-social economic systems. Graph theory provides a means of modeling ecology. And quadratic equations often used to solve economic problems related to agriculture.

Physics

The following concepts and principles of physics have been essential to the development of new technologies:

- Bernoulli's principle – states that, when the speed of an inviscid flow increases, the pressure (or potential energy) of the flow will decrease. Consequently, faster moving air creates slower static pressure and higher dynamic pressure. Carburetors and pitot tubes work on Bernoulli's principle.
- Aerodynamics – include four forces relevant to flight: thrust, lift, drag, and weight. Thrust is a reaction force explained by Newton's Second and Third Laws. When mass is accelerated in one direction, it will generate an equal force in the opposite direction. Jet engines, propeller blades, and rockets generate thrust by

pushing air in the direction opposite to flight. Lift is a force that is generated perpendicular to the oncoming air flow (using Bernoulli's Principle). Airplane wings are designed to take advantage of lift (climbing, descending, banking). Drag is a force that is generated parallel to the oncoming air flow, and opposes the motion of an object. Weight is applied by gravity. In order to achieve flight, all forces must be balanced.

Biology

Biology includes several fields with an especially strong focus on developing new technologies. One such field is biological engineering, which attempts to emulate biological system and, thereby, develop new products or enhance existing biological systems. Biological engineering is responsible for the creation of renewable bioenergy, biocompatible materials, medical devices, diagnostic equipment, and similar technologies. A second field is molecular biology. It helped create the therapies and techniques used in gene therapy, which treats diseases by inserting, altering, and removing genes within a person's cells and tissue. Using techniques developed in molecular biology, gene therapy is capable of replacing mutated genes or even modifying and correcting mutated cells. A third field is pathology, which uses laboratory equipment to diagnose disease. Another field is biotechnology, which uses living organisms and bioprocesses to create products or processes.

Chemistry

An understanding of chemistry is necessary to convert raw materials—such as oil, air, water, minerals, metals, etc.— into usable and marketable materials—

such as solvents, soaps, pesticides, cement, etc. The chemical industry consists of numerous businesses that use chemical processes and reactions to create and refine products. Below is a partial list of such products:
1. Petrochemicals – includes ethylene, propylene, benzene, and styrene.
2. Agrochemicals – includes fertilizers, insecticides, and herbicides.
3. Polymers – includes polyester, polyethylene, and Bakelite.
4. Fragrances/flavors – includes vanillin and coumarin.
1. Inorganic industrial compounds – includes ammonia, nitric acid, sodium hydroxide, and sulfuric acid.
5. Organic industrial compounds – includes phenol, urea, and ethylene oxide.
6. Ceramics – include silica brick and frit.
7. Explosives – includes ammonium nitrate, nitrocellulose, and nitroglycerin.
8. Oleochemicals – include lard and soybean oil.
9. Elastomers – includes polyisoprene, neoprene, and polyurethane.

Feasibility assessment and design requirements

The feasibility assessment phase is the third phase of the engineering design process. It determines whether or not the proposed solution is possible by asking two main questions: Is the project based on an achievable idea? Is the project within the cost constraints of the organizations? These questions are best answered by an experienced engineer with good judgment. He is arguably the most important component of this phase. If the project is feasible, it is sent through the design phase.

The design requirements phase is the fourth phase of the engineering design process. It establishes the software and hardware parameters and testability, maintainability, and other key project requirements. It is carried out concurrently with the feasibility phase.

Research and conceptualization

The research phase is the first phase of the engineering design process. It involves locating and examining information on a specific engineering issue or problem. It may require studying literature and documents on the topic and identifying existing solutions, costs, and market needs. Reverse engineering of similar market products is also a potential avenue of research. Common sources of research information include trade journals, governmental documents, local libraries, the World Wide Web, and interviews with subject matter experts.

The conceptualization phase is the second phase of the engineering design process. It involves identifying potential solutions for the problem using various techniques of ideation. One popular ideation technique is brainstorming, which involves rapidly thinking of and adopting solutions. Another technique is trigger word. One person says a word associated with the problem. Hopefully, this word evokes additional words and phrases that can be used to create solutions. Another technique is a morphological chart, which includes design characteristics of the problems. Engineers then propose solutions for each characteristic.

Detailed design

Detailed design phase is the sixth phase of the engineering design process. It provides very specific and detailed specifications (solid models and drawings) on the project. Common specifications include external marking,

design life, packaging requirements, operating parameters, test requirements, external dimensions, materials requirements, reliability requirements, external surface treatments, maintenance and testability information, and operating and non-operating environmental stimuli. CAD, or computer-aided design, programs are very helpful during this phase. They increase design efficiency through optimization, which decreases part volume while simultaneously maintaining quality. CAD programs can also perform the finite element method, which calculates stress and displacement. The engineer then determines whether or not these stresses and displacements conform to project parameters.

Preliminary design, production planning and tool design, and production design

The Preliminary design phase, also known as embodiment design, is the fifth phase of the engineering design process. It defines the overall system design—including schematics, layouts, and diagrams—in a very general way. The design will change as the project proceeds, but these early diagrams will provide guidance in the early stages. Preliminary design phases leads to the detailed design phase.

The Production planning and tool design phase is the seventh phase of the engineering design process. It establishes a plan for mass producing the product and identifies the manufacturing tools that should be used. It is during this phase that a working prototype is built and tested for standard compliance. Common tasks include material selection, production process selection, sequence of operation determination, and tool selection.

The Production phase is the eighth phases of the engineering design process. It involves manufacturing the product and conducting periodic tests of machinery.

Integrated systems and systems thinking

Integrated systems consist of numerous systems working in conjunction. Technology often consists of smaller systems combined together to form larger systems. In this way, systems are the base components of technology. Consider, for example, an automobile. It consists of numerous electronic and mechanical parts. These parts work together to create the subsystems (steering, lighting, combustion, propulsion, etc.) of which the automobile is comprised.

Systems thinking involves viewing a system as a collection of interconnected parts or processes, and then analyzing the cause and effect relationships between those parts or processes. Systems thinking is necessary when creating new products that always perform as intended.

Processes, materials, people, and capital

The following resources are required to perform technological functions:
- Processes – systematic sequences of actions through which humans create, design, invent, produce, control, maintain, and use products and systems. They are the methods through which resources are turned into products.
- Materials – include natural resources such as wood and tone; synthetic resources such as plastics, alloys, and concrete; and, mixed resources such as leather, plywood, and paper.
- People – include the manpower and labor that goes into

performing some task or function related to technology. People are arguably the most important resource.
- Capital – is necessary to create products and maintain technological systems. This resource includes money and all other financial instruments.

Technology systems and feedback

A system consists of interrelated components that work together in order to bring about a certain outcome or achieve a specific goal. Systems exist in many different forms—technological, environmental, social, etc. Some systems were created through natural processes while other systems are manmade. As a core concept of technology, systems include the following topics:
- A technology system is a manmade system. It combines materials, devices, energy, structures, and information as a means of solving problems or creating products.
- Feedback occurs when output produced by a particular event or behavior influences a recurrence of the same event or behavior in the future. There are two primary types of feedback: positive feedback, which increases the occurrence of the event or behavior that produced the output, and negative feedback, which decreases the occurrence of the event or behavior that produced the output. Systems often incorporate feedback components that allow for the system to be changed or refined.

Resources

Resources are required to carry out technological activities. The key resources in technology include the following:

- Tools and machines – devices and instruments intended to extend or improve human capabilities. Tools can be handheld or motor-driven, and often perform functions such as cutting, chopping, digging, etc. Machines are structures of moving and unmoving parts that perform work. They function by changing the application of energy. Simple machines include wheels, pulleys, screws, wedges, etc.
- Processes
- Materials
- People
- Capital
- Energy
- Time
- Information

In many cases, engineers must choose between resources. This decision will be made by analyzing tradeoffs, or the advantages and disadvantages of using one resource relative to another resource. Tradeoffs may include the cost, availability, desirability, and waste associated with a particular resource.

Energy, time and information

The following resources are required to perform technological functions:

- Energy – the ability to perform work. Technological systems input energy, and though application, convert it into a specific function or product.
- Time – must be allocated for the performance of any activity. Because time is limited and is required by all technological activities, it must be used as effectively and efficiently as possible.

- Information – includes any data that has been gleaned through reading, listening, observing, researching, or consulting any number of sources. Such data need not be factual, although facts are a type of information. Knowledge is more factual and reliable than information. When being used by technological systems, information should be arranged and presented in a rational and useful way.

Requirements

Requirements are the criteria and constraints that determine the final design and development of a system or project. They are created by examining the system in terms of concept-generation, marketing, production, use, disposability, and fiscal issues. Criteria include the parameters of the system design. They encompass the elements and features that define the system and determine the manner in which it should operate. A common criterion is the level of efficiency at which the system should function. Constraints are the limits on system design. They often reflect restrictions on funding, human capabilities, space, material, time, and the environment. Constraints tend to be relative, and must be balanced against each other based on the constraint's importance in the system design. Engineers must work within the criteria and constraints of the system design.

Quality control

Quality control makes certain that products meet design requirements and customers receive functional products. It involves setting parameters for the system or product, and then making certain the system or product operates within those parameters. Quality control is an ongoing process in which the materials that enter the system, system operation, and system output are constantly evaluated against an acceptable range. Nonconformances are then identified and corrected. The parameters used by quality control are often based on tolerances and specifications created from engineering standards and marketing research, which collects and examines customer reactions, both good and bad, that influence future designs and iterations of the project.

Processes

A process is usually a routine set of procedures through which materials are input and then converted into something more useful, such as a product, a service, or even a different process. In technology and engineering, a process is focused on completing a certain project, and is often described as a set of transformations that occur between input and output. These transformations are defined by their parameters and constraints. New processes are often the result of new technologies, which are the fruits of human creation and innovation. New processes lead to new products and systems that solve problems and enhance human capabilities. We create new technologies to make our lives easier and to increase our happiness and comfort.

Optimization and tradeoffs

Optimization is a process through which designers and engineers attempt to make a product or system as efficient and functional as possible. Optimization improves the overall system by bettering the performance of specific characteristics. Mathematical models are an important component of optimization. They help engineer to test and predict possible variations in system design.

A tradeoff occurs when one characteristic is lost in exchange for another characteristic with a different set of strengths and weaknesses. When optimizing a product, engineers are often forced to make tradeoffs, and must do so with full understanding of the consequences. For instance, in order to achieve a relatively light product weight, an engineer may be forced to use weaker materials.

ISO 9000

ISO 9000 is a set of rigorous international quality standards that are applicable to numerous types of organizations. Maintained by the International Organization for Standardization, ISO 9000 is designed to help companies improve the quality of their products, processes, and services in a systematic and continuous manner. Companies can receive an ISO 9000 certification by meeting certain requirements, including the following:

- Proper record keeping system.
- Constant evaluation of manufacturing processes to ensure the creation of quality products.
- Examination of outgoing products for defects, and taking appropriate corrective action when required.
- Method for continuous improvement.
- Regular reviews of processes and quality systems to ensure efficiency.

Although an ISO 9000 certification does not guarantee a certain level of quality within end products and services, it does guarantee that certain quality and business process are being practiced.

Application of quality control procedures to engineering and technology-related situations

Quality engineers are responsible for managing, controlling, and addressing product quality. Quality engineers make use of statistical process control tools such as control charts, which identify statistical variations within a process. SPC tools help determine the specific metrics that should be monitored and the method by which they should be sampled. By following the control limits set by these tools, employees can identify nonconforming products and correct or remove them before they pass on to the next production step or the customer. Defects in the production process should be corrected as early as possible; consequently, the quality engineer will work closely with suppliers to ensure conformance and contain potential problems. Additionally, quality engineers are engaged in continuous improvement, such as Six Sigma and lean manufacturing, which seeks to reduce statistical variation and the number of nonconforming products.

Ergonomics and ADA compliance

Ergonomics is used to create equipment and devices designed in such a way as to place the least amount of stress possible on the human body and its mental faculties. During the design process, ergonomists must identify any stressors (excessive force, unnatural postures, frequent repetition, etc.) that occur while using the equipment or device. If these stressors do not conform to ergonomic guidelines, they must be documented and their statistical variation quantified. Based on these findings, the ergonomist must determine whether there is any correlation between the nonconformances and injuries recorded while using the product, and make recommendations to the product engineers.

ADA, or the Americans with Disabilities Act, creates and publishes construction standards intended to help provide disabled persons with better access to buildings. In March 2012, all new construction must comply with ADA standards.

Research and development

Research and development, or R&D, is a systematic and creative process undertaken with the intent of improving knowledge, culture, and society, and developing new applications. R&D is often focused specifically on scientific and technological endeavors, and is carried out by both private industry and government. Most companies will not survive unless they consistently innovate and develop new technologies; consequently, companies with strong R&D departments tend to outperform those without consistent R&D departments. Pharmaceutical companies, on average, spend more on R&D than other companies. They devote much of this funding to researching mechanisms, identifying chemical compounds, proving a concept, fulfilling safety requirements, and discovering delivery methods. In some cases, different companies may form an R&D alliance, in which each party agrees to share their findings and new technology with the other parties. Businesses may form R&D alliances if they lack consistent R&D departments.

Troubleshooting technology systems

Troubleshooting procedures focus on solving problems that derive from issues other than a user's unfamiliarity with the technology system (as opposed to standard procedures, which focus on familiarizing the user with the system). Such problems include component

- 16 -

failures, unforeseen product limitations, and incompatibility. The process of troubleshooting consists of two primary phases:

- Diagnosis phase – The user must identify and describe the issues he is experiencing, such as unusually slow performance or failure to complete tasks. These issues are symptoms of underlying problems. The user diagnoses the problem by matching the symptoms to symptoms listed in the troubleshooting procedures.
- Resolution phase – After identifying the problems, the user follows a solution path. There may be multiple possible solution paths available to the user, and these paths may vary in complexity.

Diagnosis and resolution are not always separate and distinct processes. Further diagnoses may be required during the resolution phase.

Manufacturability, construction costs and consumer feedback

Manufacturability determines the ease with which a product can be manufactured. Engineers seek to design for manufacturability—that is, when designing a product, engineers always ensure that there is feasible way in which the product can be produced. Otherwise, it may fail at the manufacturing stage.

Construction costs are estimated by cost engineers, who use scientific principles and techniques. Construction costs encompass a wide array of problems, including business planning and management, project management, planning and scheduling, profitability analysis, cost estimation and cost control.

Consumer feedback can be gathered by interviews, surveys, focus groups, meetings, and many other data gathering tools. Based on feedback from these tools, engineers can recommend and incorporate design revisions that will increase the usability of new products.

Experimentation and invention

New technological innovations often lead to new business models and customer experiences that cannot be tested via conventional market research methods. Consequently, experimentation may be the only means of creating a product that will be useful to consumers and, therefore, successful on the market. Experimentation is far less predictable than established business models, but is often necessary to develop new and useful technologies, processes, services, etc.

Invention is the process by which new technologies are developed. New inventions can build off of existing technologies or they can be revolutionary, representing a radical breakthrough. Every new technology is the product of invention. The concept of invention is the basis for patent law. By applying for a patent, the inventor of a new technology can exclude others from using, selling, or importing the technology for the duration of the patent.

Models and modeling

Models are important to the design process because they help engineers and designers better visualize and understand the final product before it goes into production. There are different types of models. Physical models, for example, are physical, three-dimensional copies. They can be smaller than the products they represent (these are often used to test a specific design feature without incurring the expense of a full-sized prototype) or they can be larger (these are often used to provide a better view of smaller components that otherwise may be difficult to see). A scale model is a special type of physical model. Regardless of its size relative to the final project, a scale model is always exactly proportional. Prototypes are scale models that are the same size as the products they represent. Certain graphics software programs are capable of modeling objects in 3D. Computer modeling may be less expensive than creating a physical model while giving engineers the same benefit of visualization.

MSDS

An MSDS, or Material Safety Data Sheet, explains the properties of a specific substance, and provides a means of cataloguing substances according to their effects and risks. It is an integral component of workplace safety as it provides information necessary to the safe handling and storage of the substance. Common MSDS information includes toxicity, health effects, first reactivity, storage methods, disposal methods, protective equipment, spill-handling procedures, melting point, boiling point, flash point, and other physical data. They should be present wherever chemicals are being used or kept. MSDS data sheets are not necessarily intended for general consumers; rather, they are meant for those who work with chemicals in an occupational setting. MSDS formats differ between countries based on national requirements, and a substance should have a different MSDS data sheet for each supplier and country in which it is present.

Standard procedures

Standard procedures when working around materials and equipment related to technology include the following:

- Do not bring pets or nonessential personnel.
- Do not consume food or drink.
- Familiarize yourself with the proper operation of all equipment and materials by consulting user guides.
- Wear shoes, shirts, and all other appropriate attire.
- Tie back long hair and remove loose clothing (ties, scarves, dangling jewelry, etc.) so that they do not contact equipment or materials.
- Refrain from dropping equipment.
- Observe appropriate precautions when working around electrical equipment.
- Ensure that all equipment and instrumentation is calibrated correctly.
- Ensure that that power is off before making circuit connections.
- Power untested circuits with adjustable power sources at their lowest levels.
- Be professional in your conduct.

Fire

The following procedures should be undertaken in the event of fire:
- Sound the fire alarm if you will be unable to extinguish the fire on your own or a serious emergency has occurred, such as the release of toxic gas.
- Use a nearby fire extinguisher to extinguish the fire. If possible, extinguish the fire using CO2 units rather than dry chemical units. CO2 units often pose less risk to equipment.
- Carry a fire extinguisher with you when going to an area in which a fire might be present.
- When a person's clothing is on fire, roll them on the floor or wrap them in a coat or blanket.

- 18 -

- Immediately leave a building in which a fire alarm has been sounded.

Electrocution

The following procedures should be undertaken in the event that someone is being electrocuted:
- Never touch someone who is being electrocuted.
- Turn off power supply if possible. This can be done at the work bench or at a breaker panel.
- If the power cannot be turned off, use a piece of non-conducting material (such as lumber) to separate the person from the energized conductor.
- Ensure that the person is breathing and check for pulse. Administer CPR if necessary. Only qualified individuals should administer CPR.
- Seek medical assistance.

Whenever equipment is damaged, report it to the appropriate personnel for repair. Damaged equipment can be very hazardous. A blown fuse or circuit breaker indicates a faulty circuit; therefore, identify and correct the faulty circuit before resetting the breaker or replacing the fuse.

OSHA

OSHA, or Occupational Safety and Health Administration, is a federal regulatory agency that enforces workplace safety and health standards to prevent work-related injuries, illnesses, and fatalities. OSHA applies to most workplaces, and requires the following workplace safeguards:
1. Guards – must be placed on all moving parts where contact is possible.
2. Permissible exposure limits, or PEL – prevent chemical or dust concentrations from exceeding certain limits.
3. Personal protective equipment, or PPE – require use of respirators, gloves, coveralls, goggles, face shields, and/or other protective equipment when working in certain industrial environments.
4. Lockout/tagout – requires that energy sources be secured in an off condition when maintenance or repairs are being performed.
5. Confined space – requires air sampling and use of a buddy system while working in enclosed areas, such as tanks, pits, manholes, etc.
6. Hazard communication – requires that workers are informed of workplace chemical hazards.
7. Process safety management – lessens risk of large industrial accidents.
8. Blood borne pathogens, or BBP – prevents workers from being exposed to blood borne pathogens, such as HIV.
9. Excavations and trenches – must follow certain procedures and use certain safety equipment if they are more than five feet down.
10. Asbestos exposure – limit occupational exposure to asbestos.

Safety assessments

- A safety assessment is a method of quantifying and understanding the hazards and risks associated with certain products and materials, such as hazardous chemicals. Safety assessments incorporate multiple scientific disciplines, and typically involve professional risk assessors hired by the company. Chemical companies, consumer product companies, government agencies, insurance agencies, consulting firms, medical device manufacturers and many others make use of risk assessors. Most safety or risk assessments involve three stepsThe hazard (i.e. the consequences of exposure).

- Perform a dose-response analysis to determine the dosage necessary to produce a certain response.
- Perform exposure quantification in order to determine the dosage that the population is likely to receive.

The information gained during safety assessments should be incorporated into demonstrations, training, tests, and record keeping.

Engineering drawings

Engineering drawings are a specific type of technical representation based on the technical drawing discipline. They include and define all the requirements and critical information of a particular product, such as:

- Geometry – includes the shapes of the object and its appearance from various angles.
- Dimensions – include the size of the object expressed in standard units, such as inches, centimeters, feet, meters, etc.
- Materials – include the components of the product.
- Finish – identifies the required surface quality of the product. In most cases, products contained within industrial machines require lower surface quality than consumer products.

Based solely on the drawing, a manufacturer should be able to create the product or component in question.

Engineering drawings generally follow certain standardized conventions, such as GD&T, which mandate the use of certain layouts, nomenclatures, interpretations, typefaces, line styles, sizes, etc.

Flowcharts

Flowcharts illustrate the steps within a various algorithm or process. They offer solutions to a particular problem, and help document particularly complex processes. Flowcharts consist of various types of shapes: boxes, which contain activities; diamonds, which contain decisions the user must make; and, arrows, which represent the flow of control. Additionally, flowcharts illustrate the following types of activities: start and end, processing steps, inputs

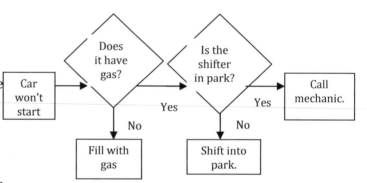

and outputs, conditionals, decisions, junctions, and connectors.

Spreadsheets, graphs, and time charts

A spreadsheet is a digital simulation of a paper accounting worksheet. There are a number of software applications capable of generating spreadsheets. It contains multiple cells with each cell containing alphanumeric text, numeric data, or a formula that defines how information within the cell will be calculated.

	A	B	C
1	100	200	150
2	50	300	250
3			

In Excel, when the formula "=SUM(A1:A2)" is entered into cell A3, it should display a value of 150.

A graph is a visual representation that conveys complex information or concepts in quickly and easily understandable ways. Examples include bar charts, pie charts, column charts, organizational charts, and flowcharts.
Time charts serve as means of planning functions and activities.

Communication

Careers

Software developer (also known as an analyst developer, developer, and programmer) examines requirements for new or modified computer applications, and translates them into program specifications. Responsibilities include designing programs, testing programs, writing programs, and using programs to solve problems. Developers often must know multiple programming languages.

Business systems analyst (also known as a business systems planner and solutions architect) identify the business and information needs within an organization, and then enhance productivity and efficiency by helping develop new IT solutions.

Database programmer (also known as a database coordinator and database administrator) is responsible for database design, implementation, maintenance, and security. Specifically, the database programmer develops the database strategy and identifies means of improving performance and capacity.

Information systems analyst (also known as an information systems designer) determines whether or not the computer system is fulfilling the organization's need in the most efficient manner possible. This position requires comprehensive knowledge of telecommunications technology, software applications, and business operations and processes.

Chief Information Officer, or CIO, leads an organization's IT group. The CIO determines how information technology can benefit the organization competitively, and reports directly to the CEO. In this position, leadership skills, business knowledge, and the ability to create and impart vision are more important than technical skills. CIOs may have an IT degree, but many simply work their way up the company ladder.

Computer engineers design, install, and perform maintenance on computer and computer equipment. They use product control techniques to enhance total system performance, and may design the complex hardware equipment that is necessary for system operation. In most cases, the position requires an electronics degree, mechanical engineering degree, or electrical engineering degree. Trade certifications are beneficial when the focus is repair work.

Web developers create, test, and maintain Web pages and links. This includes updating content (video, audio, animation, etc.), creating interactive components (search engines, chat rooms, etc.), ensuring continuous operation, creating appropriate documentation (maintenance, installation, troubleshooting, etc.), and compiling statistics. This position may require an IT or similar degree, and knowledge of HTML, programming languages, databases, and various software applications.

Telecommunication

Telecommunication describes the act of communication by transmitting information over long distances. This includes any information transmitted or received via email, instant messaging, radio, telephones, television, VoIP, and videoconferencing. The telecommunication industry provides a wide range of services, such as telephone service, broadcasting, and Internet access. Major telecommunication service providers include Verizon, AT&T, T-Mobile, Telenor, Vodafone, China Mobile, etc. Every telecommunications system

- 22 -

has three basic components: a transmitter, which converts information into a signal; a transmission medium, such as the free space channel, which carries the signal; and, a receiver, which converts the transmission into usable information. Telecommunication networks consist of many different terminals, links, and nodes that communicate between each other. Examples include computer networks, the Internet, and telephone networks.

Major service providers

Verizon Wireless is the largest US provider of wireless phone service and telecommunications networks. Key products and services include LTE (4G), SMS, MMS, V Cast (video on demand), V Cast Mobile TV, Push to Talk, AMPS, satellite phone rental and sales, Friends and Family, and On Star.

AT&T Mobility is the second largest US providers of wireless telecommunications service. Key products and services include HSPA, HSDPA, HUSPA, WCDMA, UMTS, EDGE, GPRS, and GSM.

China Mobile is a Chinese state-owned telecommunications company and the largest telecommunications and mobile phone provider in the world. Key products include mobile voice and multimedia services.

Vodafone is a British telecommunications company, the second largest in terms of subscribers and the largest in terms of revenue. Key products include fixed line and mobile telephone service, internet access, and digital television.

America Movil is a Mexican telecommunications company, the fourth largest mobile service provider in the world. Key products include fixed line and mobile telephone service, internet service, telecommunications, and cable television.

Network node, network interface cards, repeaters, bridges, and switches

A network node is any computer linked to the network. Linked computers lose their status as personal computers because they share resources.

Network interface cards enable computers to connect over a network. Each computer on the network must have an interface card with a unique ID.

Repeaters enable signals to travel farther in the network without degradation. They receive signals from the network, clean and regenerate them, and then retransmit them at a higher power level. They do not read signals, however.

Bridges first read the destination address of the signal, and then only forward it to the other network if the signal is intended for a computer on the opposite side. A bridge is more than a repeater method because two computers on the same side of the bridge can communicate without hampering communication on the other side.

Switches are similar to bridges, but are capable of connecting more than two bus networks. Each bus network extends from the switch like spokes on wheel. The switch reads each message, and only forwards it down the spoke that is linked to the target computer.

Major materials providers

Ericsson is a Swedish corporation that provides telecommunication and data communication systems with an emphasis on mobile phone technology. It is the largest mobile telecommunications vendor in the world.

Nokia is a Finnish corporation that manufactures mobile phone devices. It is the highest selling mobile phone vendor in the world.

Cisco Systems is an American corporation that designs and markets voice communication technology, networking technology, communication services, and consumer electronics.

Huawei is the largest supplier of networking and telecommunications equipment in China, and the second largest in the world, ranking second only to Ericsson.

ZTE designs and manufactures telecommunications equipment and systems. It is the second largest supplier in China, and the fourth largest in the world.

Avaya is a private company that supplies enterprise network, telephony, and call center technology.

NEC is a Japanese corporation that sells information technology and network solutions.

Server, port, RAM, and ROM

A server is a computer program that serves the needs of other computer program. It may also refer to a computer responsible for running server programs. Examples include file servers, database servers, and print servers.

A port can be either a physical interface between two computing devices (hardware) or a virtual connection between two computer programs (software).

Random-access memory, or RAM, is a part of the hard disk into which the computer can both read and write information. The term 'random-access' means that the computer can access stored data in any order independent of physical location, unlike magnetic and optical disks.

Read-only memory, or ROM, usually refers to the data stored on the computer's motherboard itself (such as the BIOS) that cannot be overwritten except in certain circumstances. This contains the basic hardware programming that allows the computer to manage the processor and other devices and run the operating system.

Router, network topology

Routers allow multiple networks to be linked across an internet (which is defined simply as network of networks) by forwarding messages. Routers are unique from other network devices because they enable each network to retain its own individual characteristics.

Network topology is the arrangement of nodes within a network, and has three basic arrangements:

- Bus network links each node in the network sequentially using a single cable.
- Star network is a centralized topography in which a central computer (also known as a switch or hub) connects all nodes and regulates network access.
- Ring network is a type of decentralized network topography in which each node links to two other nodes and the final node connects to the first node, making a ring configuration. As long as the network incorporates two-way communication, a single node failure or cable break will not bring down the entire system.

Local area network, metropolitan area network, wide area network, personal area network and BIOS

A Local Area Network, or LAN, covers a local area, such as the inside of a home or a public business. Wi-Fi can be a type of LAN.

A Metropolitan Area Network, or MAN, connects multiple LANs.

A Wide Area Network, or WAN, covers a wide outdoor area and usually serves to connect office buildings or provide public Internet access.

A Personal Area Network, or PAN, includes Wi-Fi networks, Fixed Wireless Data networks, and other small area networks. Bluetooth is a type of PAN technology.

The BIOS, or basic input/output system, is a chip that is built directly into the computer. It is known as boot firmware because it is the first program run when the computer is turned on. The main function of BIOS is loading and starting the operating system. In doing so, it initializes all computer hardware; locates software stored on peripheral devices; and, then loads and executes the software. This process is known as booting.

Primary data storage

The central processing unit, or CPU, manipulates data within the computer, and consists of three main parts:
- Arithmetic/logic unit, which carries out operations (addition, subtraction, multiplication, etc.) on data.
- Control unit, which manages machine activities.
- Register unit, which consists of registers, which are data storage cells that provide temporary information storage within the CPU. There are two types of registers: special-purpose and general-purpose.

The CPU also contains a special memory area known as cache memory, which possesses several hundred kilobytes of high-speed memory. It contains information that is needed immediately, and speeds up computer operation.

Main memory is the area in which a computer stores information. It contains both random-access memory (RAM) and read-only memory (ROM), which enables BIOS operation.
The memory bus connects the CPU to main memory, and consists of two parts—an address bus and a data bus.

Secondary data storage

Mass storage devices, such as hard disk drives, serve as secondary data storage within the computer's hierarchy. It includes any devices that provide additional memory storage, such as flash drives, compact disks, DVDs, magnetic tapes, and magnetic disks. There are two types of mass storage devices:
- On-line – The device can operate without human intervention because it is attached to the machine.
- Off-line – The device only operates after some type of human intervention, such as turning on the power or plugging the device into the correct port.

Expansion cards enhance the functionality of a computer system. They are printed circuit boards, which are inserted into expansion slots within the mother board. They can provide a variety of features, such as increased memory or capabilities that were not present before, such as sounds and graphics.

Peripheral device

A peripheral device is any electronic device that is external to the computer and attached to it in some way, such as through a wire or radio connection. Peripheral devices are not part of the system architecture, but provide either input or output functions.

A keyboard is an input device that enables the user to communicate with the CPU and software. Keyboards contain various symbols—letters, numbers, and punctuation—and control commands that the user enters simply by pressing the appropriate button, which sends a unique electrical signal to the CPU.

A monitor is an output device that displays various messages to the user, especially information entered through the keyboard. It can retrieve information stored in memory.

A mouse is an input device the user operates by moving around over a flat service and clicking buttons. Movement of the mouse corresponds to movement of a cursor displayed on the monitor. In a graphical operating system, by moving the cursor over a specific data file and clicking the buttons on the mouse, the user can access the file.

General and special-purpose registers

General-purpose registers temporarily store data that the CPU is currently using. They contain the inputs to the arithmetic/logic unit and the outputs it produces. Before the CPU can perform operations on data contained in main memory, the control unit must retrieve the data and send it to the general purpose registers. Then, the control unit informs and turns on the required circuitry within the arithmetic/logic unit and identifies the registers to which the output should be sent.

Special-purpose registers help execute programs, and come in two basic types: the instruction register and program counter. The instruction register provides temporary storage for instructions that are being executed. The program counter provides temporary storage for the address of the next instruction that will be executed, keeping track of the computer's place in the program.

Selection and maintenance of software

A user should select software programs to use or purchase based on the tasks he needs performed and the program's proficiency at carrying out that task. Additionally, the user's computer must have the requisite processing capacity to run the programs. When software fails to run on a computer, it usually falls under one of the following categories:

- The computer cannot properly install the software. Troubleshooting solutions: Ensure that the files on the drive are capable of reading the software CD. Ensure the computer is capable of running the software. Ensure the correct verification number is being entered.
- An error occurs during the software's installation. Troubleshooting solutions: Ensure the computer meets software requirements. Try installing the software when the computer is in safe mode. Examine the CD for scratches or dirt.
- The program cannot load or an error occurs during program load. Troubleshooting solutions: Check software documentation for possible tips on solving the problem. Check for the existence of patches or updates from the

developer. Close all other programs. Reboot computer at least once after program has been installed.

Selection and maintenance of hardware

Before purchasing new hardware, the user should make certain it is compatible with his computer and that it fits his need. For instance, if he requires full color copies and fax ability, he may need to purchase a top-of-the-line printer. However, if he is only printing text documents without graphics, he may opt for a less-expensive model. Some peripheral devices can be fairly easy to install, such as printers, fax machines, speakers, scanners, and similar equipment. However, installation may be more difficult for hardware that actually goes inside the computer, such as processors, expansion cards, motherboards, etc. Before opening a computer, the user should disconnect all cables connected to the back of the machine in order to avoid electrocution, and ground himself in order to avoid the dangers associated with electrostatic discharge, or ESD. Like most electronic devices, computers make extensive use of semiconducting materials, such as silicon, which are less conductive than conductor materials but more conductive than insulators.

Line, space, shape, and color

Line shows the continuous movement of a point across a surface, and is a component of two dimensional shapes, i.e. shapes drawn on paper. Lines have three basic characteristics: length, thickness, and direction.

Space describes any area allocated for a certain task. It can represent two dimensional areas, such as wall space, or three dimensional areas, such as room space. Space has three basic components: background, foreground, and middle ground. It can be either positive (space occupied by an object) or negative (space between objects).

Shape is an area that differentiates itself from the surrounding space due to a boundary or variations in value, color, or texture. Shapes can show perspective, and can be geometric (rectangular doors) or organic (natural trees) in design.

Color can be used to draw attention to a particular design component. Complementary colors are opposite each other on the color wheel, and help create contrast. Monochromatic colors are the same color in different shades.

Symmetry, typography, and layout

Symmetry is a quality of aesthetic balance or proportionality in an object. In most cases, a symmetrical object is one that has two identical sides connected as if mirror images.

Typography is the technique of creating, arranging, and modifying letters. It involves selecting typefaces, point size, line lengths, line spacing, tracking, kerning, and other illustration techniques. A typeface is a set of one or more fonts (e.g., Arial, Times New Roman, Courier) intended to bring a sense of unity and cohesion to a page. Fonts can be serif or sans serif, and proportional or monospaced.

Layout describes the arrangement and treatment of elements on a page. Layout is often determining either a grid approach or a template approach. In a grid, a set of general guidelines determine the alignment and repetition of page elements. There is not set or rigid form to which the information must conform; consequently, the guidelines are invisible to the end user. In a template, the information must conform to a very specific arrangement, which is visible to the end user.

Digital image formats

Joint photographic experts group, or JPEG, provides digital storage for pictures. It consists of a grid of pixels, which can display up to 16.7 million different color variations. Pixels are the building blocks of pictures, and are the smallest image that a screen, printer, or other output device can generate.

Tagged image file format, or TIFF, provides digital storage for scanned photographs.

Graphics interchange format, or GIF, compresses graph and graphics files, and then stores them storage digitally.

Moving picture experts group, or MPEG, compresses digital videos and animation and then stores them digitally.

Digital video interactive, or DVI, is a type of interactive video system, which is capable of processing images, text, audio, and video.

Presentation graphics software supports the creation of audience presentations. It normally includes an editing application for inserting and formatting text, an application for inserting and moving graphics, and a slide show application for displaying images that aid the speaker.

Texture, value, form, and proportion

Texture is the perception of a surface quality. Graphic designers use various drawing and painting techniques to create the illusion of a surface texture, such as soft, rough, satiny, etc.

Value, also known as tone, uses light and dark contrasts to create depth and perception within an image.

A Form is an object with three measurable dimensions: height, width, and depth. In graphic design, it is created through a variety of techniques, such as light and dark contrasts

Proportion is the size of a certain element relative to other elements in the same drawing or picture. In blueprints and similar graphic representations, it is important that all objects represented within the picture are proportional—that is, the size of each object relative to every other object should be the same in the drawing as it is in real life.

Image editing, image capture, image compression, image transfer, and image assembly

Image editing is the process of modifying images. In the field of graphic design, artists enhance and manipulate electronic images using three main types of software programs: vector graphics editors, raster graphics editors, and 3-D modelers.

Image capture involves acquiring digital images from a camera or similar vision sensor. In most cases, a device known as a frame grabber will take the analogue image and convert it into a digital image for download.

Image compression involves reducing the number of bits necessary to store a digital image. It is part of image capture.

Image transfer is the process of moving an image from one storage medium, such as a photograph, into another storage medium, such as a computer disk.

Image assembly is the process of taking parts of multiple, preexisting images, and rearranging them to create a new image.

Desktop publishing software and web page development software

Desktop publishing software is capable of creating a variety of electronic documents, including advertising copy, retail packages, newsletters, promotional displays, etc. Desktop publishing programs offer different options for layout, formatting, and graphics, and usually utilize a WYSIWYG (What You See Is What You Get) user interface, which presents an accurate digital image of the finished product. Examples include Adobe Framemaker, Quark Xpress, Corel Draw, Adobe PageMaker, and many others.

Web page development software includes applications that help users design and generate content for a website. Web page content consists of hypertext and hypermedia. Hypermedia encompasses the text, video, images, and hyperlinks that create the flow of information within a webpage. The most common markup language for web pages is hypertext markup language, or HTML. It allows users to structure and format documents on the World Wide Web. They can insert structural semantics, such as text, paragraphs, lists, menus, and online help information; embed images and objects; and, create interactive forms.

Sketching

A sketch is a freehand drawing that only gives an idea of the finished product. It is a type of diagram that aids the design process by recording and allowing designers to test ideas before more expensive work must be undertaken. Sketches provide abstract summarizations of possible design solutions. Architects make frequent use of sketches.

A drawing made by instrument, or manually, usually involves a drawing board, which is a flat surface with straight sides and right angles. The board includes a T-square, which is a straight edge that can be slid across the surface of the paper. The T-square serves a variety of functions, including drawing parallel lines and holding devices such as set squares and triangles, which aid in the drawing of angles. Drawing by instrument also involves the use of compasses, French curves, and other tools that assist in drawing various shapes and arcs.

Drafting

1. Visible lines are continuous lines which represent edges that are directly visible when viewed from a certain angle.
2. Hidden lines are lines which consist of short dashes. They represent edges that are not directly visible when viewed from a certain angle.
3. Center lines are lines which consist of alternating long and short dashes. They represent the axis of a circular component.
4. Cutting plane lines are thin lines which consist of medium dashes or thick lines which consist of alternating long and double short dashes. They are used for section views.
5. Section, or cross-hatching, lines are thin lines which represent surfaces which have cut into section views.
6. Phantom lines are thin lines which consist of alternating long and double short dashes. They represent an object which is not included in the assembly or part specifications.

Scanners, printers, and vector graphics editors

Scanners are capable of taking text printed on a page and copying it into an electronic format. As a result, printed documents can be stored and published electronically.

Printers are capable of carrying out tasks that were once performed only in print shops. This makes it far less expensive to publish and create multiple copies of documents.

A vector graphics editor is software that can create and edit simple geometric forms, including points, lines, curves and shapes. The forms are then saved in a vector graphics format, such as EPS, PDF, WMF, SVG, or VML. Vector graphics software is ideal for documents which consist of only a few pages, such as flyers or brochures. Adobe InDesign and Scribus are examples of popular vector graphics editors used in desktop publishing.

Computer-aided design

Computer-aided design, or CAD, has automated many of the tasks and techniques associated with drafting. It uses computer technology and software capable of performing two-dimensional vector-based drawing and three-dimensional solid and surface modeling. CAD software creates an environment in which designers can work. This environment includes inputs tools that assist in the process of drafting, streamlining design processes and creating documentation. Much like technical and engineering drawings which are produced through more conventional drafting processes, CAD can display materials, dimensions, tolerances, processes, and other application-specific information. CAD is often used to:

- design tools, machinery, and all types of buildings
- create detailed engineering drawings or models, including conceptual designs, product layouts, analyses, and manufacturing methods and definitions.
- design objects.

CAD has helped to reduce product development costs and decrease design cycle time.

Technical drawings

There are two basic types of technical drawings: two-dimensional representations, which rely on orthographic projection, and three-dimensional representations, which rely on 3D modeling to show the object from all possible angles. There are often two sets of technical drawings for a particular product. The first set includes working drawings, which are used during the manufacturing phase. The second set includes assembly drawings, which show how the different parts of the product are put together. Most drawings include the following views:

- Section view shows an imaginary plane that cuts through an object.
- Auxiliary view shows any surfaces of an object which do not line up with the three major axes. In essence, auxiliary views represent planes through the object which are not common planes.
- Pattern view shows the size and shape of a two-dimensional object that will eventually be folded to create a three-dimensional object.
- Exploded view
- Multiview

Multiview and exploded view

Multiview involves orthographic projection, which represents three-dimensional objects on a two-dimensional surface. Multiview is created using two basic conventions: first-angle, which shows interior surfaces, and second-angle, which shows exterior surfaces. Both use quadrants in descriptive geometry and can produce a maximum of six different pictures of an object by projecting each side onto planes that run parallel to each axis of the object.

Exploded view displays the relationships between the various components of a product as well as the order in which they should be assembled. In most cases, these components are separated by space and positioned equal distances away from their correct locations. When assembling a product based on an EVD (exploded view drawing), the user should start with the components nearest the center of the drawing and work outwards.

Architectural and engineering

Architectural drawings represent a building or building project, and use certain architectural conventions, including specific types of views, sheets sizes, measurement units and scales, annotation, and cross referencing. These views include floor plans, site plans, elevations, cross sections, isometric projections, axonometric projections, and detail drawings. Types of architectural drawings include the following:
- Presentation - explains the plan and identifies its advantages.
- Survey - represents the land, structures, and buildings.
- Record - includes past architectural influences on the current design.
- Working - includes a comprehensive set of all drawings

(location, assembly, components, engineering, etc.).

Engineering drawings convey all critical information on a product, such as its geometry (i.e. shapes and views), dimensions, tolerances, material, and finish. Engineering drawings use certain line styles (visible, hidden, center, etc.) and the following views: orthographic, auxiliary, isometric, oblique, perspective, and section.

Electronic communication

Radio waves are on the longer end (+100 m - 1 mm) of the electromagnetic spectrum. They are used to broadcast television, radio, mobile phone, and wireless networking signals, and are subject to government regulation. Radio waves transmit data through modulation and variation in their amplitude, frequency, and phases.

Microwaves are generally shorter than radio waves. They are used at low intensity levels in Wi-Fi networks and higher intensity levels in microwave ovens.

Terahertz radiation is generally shorter than microwave radiation and longer than infrared radiation. It is used in high altitude telecommunications between satellites and airplanes.
Infrared radiation is generally longer than terahertz radiation. It is used for sending remote control signals, free space optical communication, optical fiber communications, and short distance communication between computer peripherals.

The Visible light spectrum is directly above infrared radiation, and is the spectrum in which the human eye sees. Optical fiber can use the visible light waves to convey sound or image information.

The Ultraviolet spectrum is used for security marks and optical storage of information.

Parallel projection views

Parallel projection views use perspective to represent a three-dimensional object in two-dimensions on a flat piece of paper. The projection lines that run parallel on the paper also run parallel in real life. Parallel projection relies on the principle of geometry by situating the object along three axes of space (X, Y, and Z). Technical drawings often use the following types of parallel projection to represent three-dimensional objects:

- An Orthographic projection displays the object along all sides by having the parallel projection lines intersect the viewing plane at 90 degree angles.
- An Isometric projection foreshortens all three axes (X, Y, and Z) equally around the object. When drawn on paper, each axis line will be drawn at a 120 degree angle from every other axis line. This is a popular form of projection because 60 degrees angles are simple to construct using only a compass and straightedge.
- An Oblique projection is created by taking the parallel projection lines and having them intersect the viewing plane at an angle other than 90 degrees.

Tolerances, specifications, dimensions, and scale

Tolerances express the limits on a particular characteristic, such as a physical dimension (height, width, etc.), measured value of a service or product, measured value of surrounding space (temperature, elevation, etc.), and physical distances between components.

Dimensions convey the required size of the product or material that is represented in the technical drawing. Circular sizes are expressed using either diametral or radial dimensioning. Distances are expressed using either linear dimensioning or ordinate dimensioning. The functional geometry and tolerances of an object are often written in a language known as geometric dimensioning and tolerancing, or GD&T.

Specifications are the requirements that the product or material is supposed to fulfill.

Scale is the ratio at which the object in the drawing corresponds to the product in real life. The relative sizes of the objects in the drawing should be the same as they are in real life.

Database management system

A database management system, or DBMS, is a group of software applications that manage information within a database, including its creation, storage, organization, and retrieval. A DBMS ensures data integrity and regulates who can access the database and who can develop and control the information contained therein. In order to search and access information within the database, a user must submit a request using query language, which is based on a certain application protocol. This language specifies the database's organization, and the access and use of its information. A database query often includes a filter, which places a limitation on the search. A DBMS normally includes a data dictionary, which lists the names and descriptions of every data record type and the relationships between them. There are six primary types of database models: hierarchical, network, relational, distributed, object-oriented, and hypermedia. DBMSs are designed to work with each of these models.

Finding information on the Internet

A search engine is a software application that provides links to Web sites based upon information given by the user. The user simply inputs a word or phrase into the application, and it generates a list of Web sites that include the word or phrase. In order to appear in the link list, a site must be registered with the search engine. Registration occurs when the search engine is alerted of the site's existence either by the site's creator or a web crawler.
A web crawler scans the Web automatically and identifies sites for the search engine to use at a later date.

A metasearch engine inputs the word or phrase provided by the user into multiple search engines.

Video production, computer animation, 3D modeling

Video production is the process of recording, editing, and distributing a video. During preproduction the shot is planned, locations are picked, the budget is set, and the storyboard is assembled. Production involves staging the shoot, cinematography, lighting, art, effects, directing, etc. During postproduction, recorded material is logged, organized, and edited, and additions such as music, effects, and transitions are made.

Computer animation is the process of digitally creating animated images. The process is similar to stop motion: A computer screen displays an image, and then continuously replaces it with subtle variations of the same image. Computer animation can be performed using either 2D or 3D computer graphics.

3D modeling, also known as 3D rendering, is the process of digitally generating a three dimensional representation of an object. Examples of 3D modeling processes include polygonal modeling, NURBS modeling, splines and patches, primitives, and sculpt modeling.

Digital imaging, audio mixing and web development

Digital imaging is the process of creating digital graphics and images. It entails processing, compression, storage and display. Digital images can be created from analogue mediums, such as photographs, and non-visual mediums, such as technical data and mathematic models.

Audio mixing is the process of combining multiple recorded sounds into one or more channels. It often involves adding effects such as reverb and changing the level, frequency content, dynamics, and panoramic position of source signal. This can be done through a mixing console or a digital audio workstation.

Web development is the process of designing a website, and includes a variety of tasks and functions, such as web design, writing markup, coding, web content development, web server configuration, network security configuration and scripting.

Geometric Dimensioning and Tolerancing (GDT) symbols

<u>Key GDT Symbols</u>
   O   **Circularity** – a form in which all points on a surface of revolution (cylinder, cone, or sphere) are the same distance from a common center or axis.
   ⊥   **Perpendicularity** – an orientation in which two lines or planes intersect at an axis of ninety degrees.
       Position – a tolerance limit at which a center or axis may vary from the exact position
   ◎   **Concentricity** – a condition in which multiple features share the same axis point.

- 33 -

ⓜ **Maximum Material Condition** –
a condition in which the size of a material
is at its maximum limit relative to the size
of a feature. For instance, a hole will not
accommodate a shaft size any larger than
is already being used.

Ⓛ **Least Material Condition** – is a
condition in which the size of a material is
at its minimum limited relative to the size
of a feature. For instance, a hole will not
accommodate a shaft size any smaller
than is already being used.

Manufacturing

Careers

Manufacturing engineers improve and streamline the production process by designing manufacturing equipment and systems and finding ways to lower costs and increase profitability.

Automation technicians are responsible for creating, installing and repairing automated systems and equipment.

Industrial designers create designs and improve existing models for a variety of manufactured products, especially commercial, medical, and industrial goods.

Quality control engineers improve the quality of manufactured products. They examine statistical data and find ways to improve product specifications.

Product engineers help design manufactured products. They conduct surveys, talk with customers, and collaborate with other members of the organization as a means of improving product design.

Product safety technicians test products to ensure compliance with safety regulations. These regulations are focused on the mechanical, electrical, and environmental operation of the product.

Manufacturing technicians repair production equipment and facilitate proper equipment functionality. They are integral in maintaining the manufacturing line.

Manufacturing industries

Manufacturing includes the following industries:

1. Beverage manufacturing – includes non-alcoholic beverages and alcoholic beverages produced through fermentation of distillation.
2. Tobacco manufacturing – includes the creation of tobacco products as well as the stemming and re-drying of tobacco.
3. Leather and allied manufacturing – produces footwear, tanning, and finishing.
4. Wood manufacturing – includes sawmills, wood preservation, veneer, plywood, and similar wood products.
5. Paper manufacturing – creates pulp, paper, paperboard and other paper products.
6. Printing and support manufacturing – includes newspapers, books, cards, stationary, and other print products. It also includes support services, such as data imaging, platemaking, and bookbinding.
7. Furniture manufacturing – creates furniture products from wood, metal, glass and similar materials.
8. Electrical equipment, appliance, and component manufacturing – creates electrical equipment, household appliances and electrical components.
9. Metal manufacturing – includes iron, steel, aluminum, ferroalloy, aluminum products and mills.

Additional industries in manufacturing

Manufacturing includes the following industries:

1. Transportation equipment manufacturing – creates vehicles, ships, railroad stock, and products related to transport of goods and people.
2. Food manufacturing – helps change livestock and agricultural

products into consumable products.

3. Petroleum and coal products manufacturing – uses processes which convert raw petroleum and coal into consumer products.
4. Computer and electronic equipment manufacturing – creates computers, peripherals, semiconductors, electrical devices, measuring devices and similar electronic devices.
5. Apparel manufacturing – encompasses two types of businesses: those that knit fabric and then cut and sew it into garments, and those that purchase fabric and then cut and sew it into garments.
6. Chemical manufacturing – turns raw materials into soap, resins, pharmaceuticals, fertilizer, pesticides, and other usable products.
7. Plastics and rubber manufacturing – transforms plastic and raw rubber into usable products.
8. Textile mills – produces yarn and fabric.
9. Textile product mills – produces textile products other than apparel.
10. Machinery manufacturing – creates products that generate mechanical force, such as equipment related to mining, turbines and metal working.

Just-in-time, continuous flow manufacturing and takt time

Just-in-time, or JIT, is lean manufacturing technique. It lowers costs and increases profit by reducing or eliminating excess inventory. During procurement, a purchased product is scheduled and received in such a way that inventory levels remain at almost zero.

Continuous flow manufacturing, or CFM, is a lean manufacturing technique. It holds that the manufacturing process should produce one piece of material at a time and at a rate determined by customer needs (i.e. takt). It normally includes the following characteristics: poka-yoke (a device or procedure that prevents defects or mistakes from moving to the next step), source inspection, self-checking, successive checks and total productive maintenance.

Takt time is part of lean manufacturing, specifically continuous flow manufacturing (CFM).

Takt time = available production time / rate of customer demand

In CFM, the single-piece flow of materials occurs in a rigid sequence of production steps with various techniques designed to minimize defects. This sequence should form a straight line or U-shaped cells.

Intermittent manufacturing, custom manufacturing, automated manufacturing and kaizen

Intermittent manufacturing produces only those goods necessary to fulfill customer orders, not to keep in stock. It normally includes the following characteristics: flexible production facilities, products made in small amounts, process-arrangement of machines and equipment, unbalanced workloads, large in-process inventory and highly skilled workers.

Custom manufacturing produces goods for a specific person or purpose.

Automated manufacturing relies on automated machines and equipment to create products. It is closely associated with factory production. Characteristics of automated manufacturing include the following: short lead times, product

- 36 -

simplifications, better quality and greater consistency.

Kaizen is a Japanese word meaning continuous improvement. It involves management in improving operation; focuses on quality; and, uses PDCA improvement cycles. Although kaizen generally occurs on a slow, incremental basis, it can be sped up through a technique known as the kaizen blitz, which uses cross-functional teams to causes rapid workplace improvement.

Resource management, manufacturing process management and enterprise resource planning

Resource management is responsible for identifying and providing the resources necessary to carry out organizational functions. Resources encompass money, personnel, inventory, human skills, equipment, machinery, and information technology. One aspect of resource management is human resources, which allocates personnel to various department and jobs.

Manufacturing process management determines the methods and processes by which products are manufactured. Its goal is increasing efficiency by reducing lead times, using smaller inventories, and reducing production time. Manufacturing process mangers often seek more efficient alternatives to the current production process.

Enterprise resource planning, or ERP, integrates all business functions and manages the flow of information between those functions and people within the organization and between the organization and its stakeholders. This information includes both external and internal resources, such as human resources, tangible assets, manufacturing, financial assets and materials. ERP often relies on specialized software.

Federal regulations and product recall

Safety and health is regulated by the following federal agencies:
- Occupational Health and Safety Administration (OSHA) – enforces worker safety regulations such as eye and ear protection, fire protection and equipment operation.
- Food and Drug Administration (FDA) – regulates new products released to the public, especially food, cosmetics, pharmaceutical drugs and health supplements.
- US Consumer Product Safety Commission (CPSC) – protects consumers against any products that pose unreasonable injury risks.
- Environmental Protection Agency (EPA) – enforces federal laws protecting land, air and water.
- US Department of Agriculture – regulates meat, poultry and eggs.

A product recall occurs when a company requests that consumers return a defective or potentially harmful batch or production run of a product. It is done to limit liability and prevent bad publicity. Product recalls can be made either voluntarily or at the compulsion of consumer protection laws or federal agencies.

5S programs, total productive maintenance and SMED

5S programs are structured around five basic principles, all of which start with the letter S:
1. Sort – separate out and eliminate unnecessary items.
2. Straighten – put all items in their proper places.
3. Scrub – clean the workplace.
4. Systematize – standardize a routine for cleaning and checking.

5. Sustain – carry out and improve on previous four steps

The goals of 5S programs are organizing the workplace, eliminating muda (Japanese for waste), creating standardized conditions and keeping discipline.

Total productive maintenance, or TPM, increases equipment effectiveness by implementing coordinated group activities and involving all operators in machine inspections, routine maintenance and repair.

Single Minute Exchange of Die, or SMED, increases production efficiency by drastically reducing setup change times— or the length of time required to changeover production machinery. It divides changes into two conditions: external setup operations, which include the changeover activities which can be performed prior to shutting down machinery, and internal setup operations, which include the changeover activities which must be performed while the machinery is shut down.

Supply chain management

Supply chain management, or SCM, oversees the entire production process, including raw material acquisition, inventory maintenance, manufacturing of goods and services and their delivery to consumers. SCM encompasses the network of businesses involved in this process. At the organizational level, SCM personnel are responsible for handling supply chain interactions, supplier relationships and business processes. They may use specialized software capable of managing inventory, good receipts, the warehouse, suppliers and sourcing, processing customer requirements and purchases orders, and using integration technology to carry out electronic transactions with supply chain partners. SCM also conducts forecasting and consumption analysis, which seeks to find a balance between supply and demand, make business processes more efficient and predict future needs.

Labeling requirements, warranty and consumer protection laws

Labeling requirements are imposed by federal agencies, such as the FDA, Federal Trade Commission, and Department of Agriculture. Labels are intended to educate the consumer on the contents and characteristics of the product or service before it is purchased.

A warranty is a promise between the seller and buyer. The seller promises that the product will meet or fulfill certain conditions, and if it fails to meet these conditions, the buyer may seek some promised remediation. Warranties can be either express (the seller openly acknowledges the warranty) or implied (it exists regardless of whether or not the seller acknowledges it). Examples of implied warranties include warrant of merchantability and warranty of fitness for a particular purpose.

Consumer protection laws protect consumers against harmful or unlawful business practices, and prevent fraudulent businesses from gaining an unfair competitive advantage.

Trade secret, patent, copyright, and trademark

A trade secret is confidential information through which a business gains a competitive advantage. Access to trade secrets is generally very restricted. They can include instruments, designs, formulas, practices and similar types of data.

A patent is an exclusive right that allows inventors to protect their inventions from

- 38 -

being copied. A patent is granted by the government in exchange for public disclosure of the invention so that others may use and make it with the patent owner's permission. Once the patent expires, anyone can copy it legally.

A copyright is an exclusive right that protects expression of an idea. It prevents anyone from copying, distributing, or adapting an original work except its creator. Copyrights are seldom registered; rather, they come about once the work is created, and apply for a limited time period.

A trademark is a unique sign developed and used by a business, such as a company logo. By stamping products with its trademark, the business can distinguish them from competitor products.

Finishing, hardening, annealing, normalizing and tempering

Finishing involves changing or coating the surface of a material in order to protect or beautify it. For instance, wooden decks are often coated with sealant as a protection from the elements.

Hardening increases the hardness of a metal by heating and then rapidly cooling it. This increases internal stresses and, thereby, increases the metal's strength (resistance to deformation) while making it more brittle and reducing its toughness.

Annealing softens a metal by heating and then slowly cooling it. This lessens internal stresses and, thereby, decreases the metal's brittleness and increases its toughness, malleability and ductility (its ability to be shaped, stamped and worked on further).

Tempering is a heat treatment that increases the metal's toughness, decreases its hardness and cracking, and makes it more malleable and ductile.

Normalizing is a heat treatment that returns the metal to its near-equilibrium state. It strikes a balance between strength and hardness.

Rapid prototyping and manufacturing

Rapid prototyping is an aspect of computer-aided manufacturing. It relies on additive manufacturing technology to automate the creation of models, prototypes, and other types of objects. Rapid prototyping is now capable of producing limited numbers of parts that can be used in assembly of the actual product. Additive manufacturing technology is capable of assembling parts in layers based on 3D model information.

Rapid manufacturing, also known as direct digital manufacturing, involves producing parts based on information contained in CAD or additive manufacturing files. Rapid manufacturing can makes use of most alloy metals as well as different types of polymers. It has applications in a variety of industries, especially automotive, dental, fashion, medical, and any other industry in which midsized complex parts are prevalent.

Casting, forming, separating, conditioning and assembling

Casting involves pouring a molten or liquid material (such as metal, concrete, plaster or clay) into a mold, and then letting it solidify into the shape determined by the mold. Casting is useful for forming complex shapes.

Forming involves shaping a material using a die and external force. For instance, a person can shape a piece of clay by forming it around a metal cylinder.

Separating involves removing excess material from an object in order to create size and shape. For instance, scissors can cut into a piece of fabric and, thereby, alter its size and shape.

Conditioning involves applying heat, pressure or chemical reactions in order to change the properties of a material. For instance, pottery is baked as means of hardening it.

Assembling involves fastening, bonding, or otherwise joining two pieces together, either permanently or temporarily. For instance, pieces of a plastic model are often glued together.

Computer-aided manufacturing and robotics

Computer-aided manufacturing, or CAM, relies on computer software to augment the manufacturing process in some way. Its goal is increasing the efficiency, accuracy, consistency and speed with which products are created. CAM software may guide the tools and machinery that create the products, or it may help coordinate management, planning and other plant operations. CAM can control every step in the production process, from the processing of raw materials to their conversion into consumable products.

Robotics is an aspect of computer-aided manufacturing. Robots are capable of automating certain manufacturing tasks, and are most prevalent with the automobile manufacturing industry. The most common manufacturing application for robots is materials handling, which involves moving materials and components with the factory. The second most common application is spot welding. More recently, robots have started performing lighter tasks, such as parts installation, packaging (e.g., foods and

electronics), and service jobs (e.g., automatic tellers and checkouts).

Wood

Wood is used heavily within the manufacturing industries, which uses a variety of natural wood and engineered wood products, such as plywood. Plywood is also formed from sheets of timber glued together. It possesses strong resistance to breaking, shrinkage, warping and cracking. Plywood can be made from softwood, such as pine and fir, or hardwood such as birch. Softwood plywood is used prominently in furniture and house construction, including walls, floors, roofs, fences and wind bracing panels. Hardwood plywood is very strong and resistant, and is used for the most demanding construction applications, such as heavily-trafficked floors, scaffolding, concrete formwork system panels, etc. Wood products are often less expense and better for the environment than other materials, such as steel or concrete.

Masonry materials

Masonry materials include bricks, concrete blocks, stone, marble, travertine, limestone, glass, stucco, tile and granite. In masonry, these materials are stacked and bound together into structures. The binding material is known as mortar. Masonry construction has very high compressive strength (the ability to support weight vertically), but lacks in tensile strength (the ability to withstand twisting and stretching). It is resistant to heat, fire, and projectile impact, but is susceptible to weather wear and requires a strong foundation to support its weight. Masonry uses the following tools:

- ◆ Masonry trowel – used to level, shape, and spread mortar or concrete.

- ◆ Joint filler – a compressible material, such as rubber, that is used to fill and keep dry the joints between structural members.
- ◆ Hawk – holds the mortar or joint compound as it is being applied.
- ◆ Bricklayers hammer – used during bricklaying.
- ◆ Bull float – used to smooth the surface of concrete.

Plastics

Plastics are a synthetic polymer created from petroleum and natural gas. There are two basic types of plastics: thermoplastics, which can be remolded numerous times, and thermosetting plastics, which undergo irreversible curing. Numerous everyday products are created from plastics, such as grocery bags, storage bags, bottles, jars, food packaging, milk jugs, flooring, window frames, film, polyester fibers, textiles, pipes, gutters, show curtains, lights, straws, household appliances, furniture, siding, dish ware, utensils, tooth brushes, automobile components, and many more. Plastics are fairly inexpensive and easily produced; however, they pose several environmental concerns. They emit pollutants such as greenhouse gases and accumulate in landfills and ocean gyres. Because they are created from a nonrenewable resource (petroleum), their cost will rise as the resource is depleted, and the cost of other petroleum-based products, such as gasoline, will also rise.

Metal alloys

Metal alloys have many different manufacturing applications, ranging from construction to surgical equipment. One of the most commonly used metals is steel, which is produced by alloying iron with carbon—though other materials may be used as well. The tensile strength, hardness, and ductility of steel depend on the amount of carbon within it. Increased levels of carbon increases the alloys hardness while decreasing its ductility (i.e. the alloy is less resistant to twisting and warping). Long steel is used in the creation of high-strength wire, bridges, and building structures. Flat carbon steel is used in major appliances as well as automobiles and boats. Stainless steel is used in mechanical equipment, surgical equipment, and cutting tools. Other common manufacturing metals include aluminum alloys, which feature prominently in the aerospace, shipbuilding, cycling and automotive industries.

Composites

A composite consists of multiple materials that differ widely in their properties and characteristics. Composites can be naturally-occurring, such as wood, or manmade, such as engineered wood, fiberglass and concrete. Fiberglass combines plastic and thin fibers of glass, which provide structural reinforcement. It is lightweight while possessing good tension and compression strength. Fiberglass is used prominently in the manufacturing of storage tanks, pipes, houses, cars, and boats. Concrete is used in a variety of construction applications, but poses several environmental concerns. For instance, paved roadways are one of the major causes of the urban heat island effect, in which a city tends to be hotter than its surrounding area. Concrete surfaces also lead to increased surface runoff, which causes erosion. Additionally, the manufacture of concrete releases carbon dioxide, a greenhouse gas.

Construction

Careers

Civil engineering technicians assist engineers, architects, and planners in planning, designing, locating and constructing buildings. They estimate material costs and amounts, perform quality control inspections on materials, and conduct suitability tests on soil, concrete, and building materials.

Building inspectors ensure that the structure complies with all applicable codes, such as building, plumbing, electrical and mechanical codes.

Safety specialists maintain safe environments within construction areas. They make sure that hazardous waste is disposed of properly, perform routine inspections on equipment and scaffolding, conduct safety education classes, consult with managers and engineers, and write safety reports.

Site managers ensure that a building project does not exceed budget or the time schedule. They handle any delays, problems, and communication between parties. They are also involved in quality control.

Contractors supervise the entire construction process including the construction of work spaces, homes, schools and other buildings. They write contracts, make bids, estimate costs, perform scheduling, manage labor and ensure safe storage of equipment and construction materials.

Types of construction

Light construction describes light frame construction, which is limited to floor and ceiling joists, rafters and wood stud walls.

Light construction is mostly residential; however, it can apply to smaller commercial buildings that do not exceed two stories.

Heavy construction applies to any construction that uses cranes, excavators, and other large machines.

Civil construction applies to the construction of social infrastructure, such as bridges, dams, irrigation projects, air field surfacing and grazing, sewer and water lines, highways, roadways, sidewalks, curbs, and railroads. In some definitions, heavy construction and civil construction are combined into a single category.

Industrial construction applies to the construction of factories, manufacturing facilities, power plants and processing plants. It requires extensive planning and teams of people with specialized skills in design and construction. Big industrial corporations carry out the majority of industrial construction projects.

Building codes

Building codes are a set of construction standards that determine the manner in which structures are built and repaired. Building codes are established and enforced at the municipal level. They regulate building materials and workmanship quality, such as electrical wiring, sanitation facilities, fire and safety equipment, and similar building aspects. City officials conduct building inspections in order to ensure compliance. If compliance is met, the official will issue a certificate of occupancy, also known as an occupancy permit. This document explains the proper use of the building in sheltering people, animals and property. For instance, in a single-family home, many building codes require an occupancy separation between the living space and the garage, in which flammable

Copyright © Mometrix Media. You have been licensed one copy of this document for personal use only. Any other reproduction or redistribution is strictly prohibited. All rights reserved.

substances are kept. If a building has multiple uses (e.g., residential and commercial), building codes usually require that builders place fire barriers, such as fire doors and fire stops, between individual occupancies.

Federal environmental regulations

The Clean Air Act of 1970 regulates the emission of six pollutants—carbon monoxide, ozone, lead, sulfur dioxide, nitrogen dioxide, and particulate matter—according to the limits established by the national ambient air quality standards, or NAAQS.

The Clean Air Act Amendment of 1990 regulates 189 additional toxic air pollutants.

The Clean Water Act, or CWA, regulates the quality and pollution content of all navigable waters in the US, including lakes, rivers, streams, wetlands, ponds, territorial seas and every other small or large body of water. Point source of water pollutions—such has construction sites, factories, and plants—must acquire a national pollution discharge eliminations system, or NPDES, permit through their state regulatory agencies.

The Wilderness Act established the national wilderness preservation system, and forbids any road construction, settlement, mechanized transportation, or other forms of development within the boundaries of the system.

The Resource Conservation and Recovery Act, or RCRA, regulates industrial waste and the manner in which it is generated, stored, treated, transported and disposed of.
The Endangered Species Act, or ESA, protects threatened or endangered species and their ecosystems on public and private land.

Permits

Permits empower their holders to carry out certain development and construction activities. Permits are usually granted by a government agency, such as the zoning board of appeals, which usually conduct a review of some sort before agreeing to the permit. There are many different types of permits. Conditional-use permits, also known as special-use permits, allow for land uses in zones where such land uses may be forbidden under existing ordinances but is generally considered for the common good. For instance, a planner may acquire a conditional-use permit in order to build residencies in an industrial zone. Nonconforming use permits are generally granted to structures that do not conform to current zoning ordinances because they were built before the ordinances were passed. Variance permits enable a landowner to use his property in a way that directly conflicts with zoning laws. A right of way is a granted by a private landowner. It empowers an agency or individual to use the landowner's property to build or maintain a road, pathway, or utility line.

Zoning

Zoning ordinances determine the manner in which land can be used in a particular community. They are designed to maintain public safety and promote public welfare. They are established and enforced by city governments via enabling acts. Zoning ordinances generally divide the community into multiple land-use districts and regulate district use, district size, the kinds of buildings that can be built, building height, setback distance (distance between the structure and streets and walkways), architecture and density (land to structure ratio). Urban areas tend to be high-density. Low density ordinances increase the space between buildings, but contribute to urban sprawl. Most zoning districts are classified as residential, industrial, commercial or agricultural. Zoning ordinances normally contain general provisions, definitions, maps, zoning district delineation and guidelines for enforcement and administration.

Zoning methods

Euclidean zoning divides a community into separate land use districts and then limits the kind of development which occurs within each district. Land use districts are designated according to the following uses: residential for single families, residential for multiple families, industrial, and commercial. A single district cannot mix land uses. Euclidean II zoning allows for mixed land uses within a single district.

Cumulative zoning allows a single land use district to combine less intensive land uses, such as residential, with more intensive land uses, such as commercial. The only stipulation is that residences can only be mixed with light industrial uses (high-tech, warehouses, and other non-polluting industries). Heavy industrial uses must remain by themselves.

Exclusive, or non-cumulative, zoning is the dominant contemporary zoning method. It forbids a land use district from incorporating any developments which do not conform to its designated use. Exclusive zoning allows for more excess room than cumulative zoning; consequently, existing businesses have more room for expansion.

Transect zoning divides the development area into six zones. The first zone is the wilderness area. Each subsequent zone is progressively more urbanized. The sixth and final zone is the urban core. Transect-based ordinances encourage mixed land uses within districts, and regulate parking placement, street layout, building height, setback, façade and design.

Overlay zoning superimposes a new zone on top of an existing land use zone and imposes additional requirements and standards.

Floating zones are unmapped zoning districts. They enable municipalities to promote certain land uses (apartments, research campuses, etc.) without actually reserving an area of land for such a use.

Cluster zoning imposes strict density standards on development, but allows flexibility in setting lot size, setback distances, various characteristics related to individual house lots, street layout, utility sites, and building placement. In cluster zoning, developers can reserve a single high-density area for residences, and leave large amounts of open space for uses such as agriculture, recreation, and preservation.

Rezoning, upzoning, downzoning, variance and extraterritorial jurisdiction

Rezoning is the act of changing the zoning classification of a land use district.

Upzoning is a type of rezoning in which higher density developments are allowed within a land use district.

Downzoning refers to two possible actions: reducing the intensity of development that is allowable within a specific land use district, or increasing the intensity of development so that higher order development is allowed within a land use district. When intensity is reduced, minimum lot sizes are often increased.

Variances allow land uses within particular district that are otherwise forbidden under existing zoning ordinances. Variances are not allowed unless an area of land is caused considerable hardship without the land use.

Extraterritorial jurisdiction, or ETJ, is the power of a municipality to enforce zoning ordinances outside its jurisdiction. It is granted by the state.

Urban analysis

An urban analysis helps determine the kind of development that best fits a certain site. It considers the context and characteristics of a location, and identifies the urban design strategies and concepts which are best suited for the construction project. There are six types of urban analysis:
- Community – examines census and demographic information, previous planning information from past projects, and the wants and needs of the general public.
- Continuity – examines the developments patterns (e.g., buildings that are unique to the community) and changes that have occurred within the community throughout its history.
- Character – examines a community's urban form, topography, views, open space, population centers, architectural character, streetscape, and environmental issues.
- Connections – determines the accessibility of a community by examining its streets, rights-of-way, parking, traffic problems, transit service, and bicycle and pedestrian services.
- Regulations and ownership.
- Economic and market setting.

Construction financing

Private Sources

- Private equity comes from individuals and corporations.
- Banks provide loans for construction, such as mortgages. Investment banks offer equity financing.
- Credit companies offer equity financing.
- Real estate investment trusts are groups of developers, lenders and equity investors who pay out over 90 percent of their earnings so that they can avoid corporate income taxes.
- Pension funds provide both debt and equity financing.
- Life insurance companies provide both debt and equity financing.

Public Sources
- Tax increment financing is focused primarily on redevelopment and infrastructure, and it may assist developers as well.
- Special service and assessment areas are special tax districts in which new residents assume most of the financial burden.
- Historic tax credits are available for restoring certified historic structures.
- Tax-exempt bonds offer low-interest loans to industrial and low-income housing developers.
- Home investment partnership program funds are provided to municipalities, who give them to developers for the purposes of building affordable housing.

Land use regulation

Quota systems place restrictions on the building permits that developers can acquire over a year. The restrictions include both the number and type of permits. Quota systems slow the future growth of communities and allow more time to assimilate existing growth. Quota systems are common in rapidly growing areas.

Moratorium restricts or completely stops certain types of development until a more thorough plan can be developed and put in place. This plan must address the expansions of water, utilities, and other necessities.

Cost is the property's value after improvements (i.e. buildings) have been added to it. Cost does not necessarily reflect the property's market value.

Cost-benefit analysis is used to determine which proposed development will generate more value in the future. It compares the benefits and costs of each proposed development.

Urban analysis

Economic and market setting analysis examines economic factors that may affect development. The factors include the current state and needs of the local real estate market; the existing market demand for certain land uses and land uses that need to be fulfilled (more office space, additional housing units, factories, etc.); available financing options (banks, tax credits, bonds, etc.); fiscal analysis of the community; and construction projects that are currently going on or have been recently approved.

Regulations and ownership examines zoning and land use regulations, design guidelines, and property ownership, including property boundaries, shapes, sizes and parcel distribution. Design guidelines include windows, doors, building types, signage, roof shapes, planting and other construction elements.

Design guidelines are often set by the community, and can be determined by studying drawings and photographs.

Construction site management

Managing a construction site involves the following tasks:

1. Supervising, coordinating, and scheduling every design and construction process throughout the project's lifetime, from its inception to the final phases. This includes meeting with owners, engineers, architects and other important personnel.
2. Determining the material, tools and labor requirements of the project. Finding the best way to acquire the necessary tools and materials, and overseeing their delivery. Hiring and dismissing workers if necessary.
3. Estimating all costs necessary to complete the project.
4. Choosing, hiring, and overseeing carpenters, plumbers, electricians, metalworkers, roofers and other specialty trade contractors.
5. Ensuring the project stays on time and within budget.
6. Overseeing site preparation, which involves clearing and excavating the land, building roads, landscaping and installing sewage systems.
7. Overseeing building construction, which involves laying foundation and building the structural framework, floors, walls and roofs.
8. Overseeing building system installation, such as fire suppression, electrical, HVAC, and plumbing systems.
9. Ensuring compliance with building codes and any other regulations. Acquiring all required building permits and

licenses. Scheduling required inspections.

10. Ensuring worker safety.

Construction project inspections

Before a building can receive an occupancy permit, it must receive the following inspections:

1. Public work inspections – ensure compliance with government contracts. Public works include sewer systems, bridges, dams, highways, and streets for compliance with government regulation.
2. Building inspection – ensures compliance with applicable building codes. It occurs in stages throughout the construction process. Building inspectors examine the following: building plans; soil, including the position and depth of the footings; the foundation after it has been poured; fire suppression system, including sprinklers, alarms, smoke control, and exits; and the completed building.
3. Electrical inspections – ensure compliance with electrical codes and standards. The main panel, subpanels, junction boxes and all wiring must be completed before an inspection can take place.
4. Elevator inspections – check all lifting and conveying devices.
5. Mechanical inspections – check all systems and equipment related to heating, air conditioning, ventilation and refrigeration.
6. Plumbing inspections – examine the layout of the piping, venting, backflow protection, and fixture settings. They ensure safe drinking water and sanitary waste disposal.

Structures

An arch is a structure that supports weight atop an open space, such as the top of a window. It normally has a semicircular shape, but can also have a flat or pointed shape. Arches remove tensile stress, and support the entire load as compressive stress.

A cantilever is a projecting structure that receives support at only one end and carries a load at the other end. Examples include diving boards and balconies.

A suspension is a structure that consists of cables supporting a horizontal beam, such as a suspension bridge. The cables are hung from a long, very strong steel cable that is attached to support columns. The structure is supported by tension in the cables and compression in the columns.

A truss is a triangular structure formed by straight beams. A node is formed where the ends of the beams connect. The node is also where tensile or compressive forces are absorbed. In a planar truss, the beams form a two dimensional plan. In a space truss, the beams create a three dimensional structure.

Steel and plumbing system

Steel possesses better compressive strength and far more tensile strength than concrete; however, steel is also far more expensive. Steel is stronger and more resistant to rust than most other metals—though its strength depends heavily on the materials with which it has been alloyed. Steel provides the support skeleton for most large buildings, such as skyscrapers. It also reinforces masonry walls, and is used in railroad track construction. The steel industry is one of the leading producers of greenhouse gases.

The plumbing system within a building consists of water supply lines, which provide usable water, and drain and vent lines, which remove waste. Water supply pipes are created from nontoxic materials, such as plastic, brass, or copper. Drain pipes are usually created from plastic, steel, cast-iron, or lead. Lead is toxic and, therefore, cannot be used in water supply lines. Pipes are often joined using a welder, which creates a bond via some molten material.

Wood and concrete

Wood is a common building material. In construction, it is found in both its natural state and as an engineered product, such as glue laminated timber. Glue laminated timber consists of several layers of timber glued together into a single, large beam. It is stronger than most forms of solid timber, and is capable of serving as a support beam within a structure. Engineered wood requires smaller diameter trees, which can be farmed. This preserves natural forests.

Concrete is made from cement, cementitious materials, water and chemicals. It is inexpensive compared to other building materials, and is used in the construction of roads, parking lots, foundations, and block walls. Concrete can carry very heavy loads (high compressive strength), but has a very low resistance to stretching and twisting (low tensile strength); consequently, concrete structures are often reinforced with steel. Concrete is also very susceptible to thermal expansion, which causes it to shrink and crack as it ages.

Structural determination

Urban development plans lay out the construction strategies for high-density urban development. Most construction incorporates the following elements: public spaces; restoration of old neighborhoods; compact design, which connects commercial and residential areas; good transit systems; walkways that encourage walking and bike riding; infill development rather than expansion; land use that improves the health and economic well-being of the poor; and affordable housing.

Suburban development plans lay out the construction strategies for low-density, homogenous suburban areas, which normally include single-family detached dwellings, office parks, retail centers, employment centers, and recreation areas. These plans facilitate automobile usage and allow for curving streets, lawns, garages, driveways and parking lots

Capital facilities plans lay out the construction strategies for roads, bridges and sewer lines within a community over a 5 to 6 year period.

Parks and open space plans lay out the construction strategies for park and open space systems, such as play grounds, parks, athletic facilities, community gardens and recreation parks.

Electrical wiring system

Electrical wires usually consist of conductors that are twisted together and encased in insulating material. The voltage requirements determine the number of conductors that must be twisted together in a single wire. Two common conductors used in electrical systems are copper and aluminum. Copper is more expensive but poses fewer problems than aluminum. Copper is the most popular choice in residential structures. Aluminum is lighter, cheaper, and better suited to larger wires and circuits. In today's electrical systems, insulation is made from synthetic materials, such as thermoplastic and polymers that act and feel like rubber.

The latter has an extremely high resistance to moisture, making it ideal for industrial and utility usage. According to most building codes, electrical systems must be firestopped, with sealing closing opening and joints, or fireproofed, which involves increasing the resistance of materials to fire. A building's electrical system includes junction boxes, through which electrical power can be rerouted.

Energy, Power, and Transportation

Careers

Energy and power technology are continuously expanding careers. There are always jobs available for individuals who want to maintain and repair power station equipment, like substations, relays, and transformers. Power dispatchers monitor electricity dispersal to guard against overloads and insufficiencies. A nuclear plant operator tests and calibrates equipment and ensures that safety guidelines are being followed. There are also many jobs, like electrical lineman, that involve installation and maintenance of equipment used to deliver electricity. Increasingly, there are abundant and lucrative career opportunities in green energy technology. All of these jobs require specialized education and training, but they can never be outsourced and will continue to offer excellent pay and intellectual stimulation.

Renewable and nonrenewable energy resources

Scientists distinguish between renewable energy resources, which can be replaced in a relatively short time, and nonrenewable energy resources, which cannot. Fossil fuels are considered nonrenewable energy resources because they take so long to form. Indeed, the rate of consumption of fossil fuels vastly outstrips the rate of new fossil fuel formation. This is one of the reasons scientists are desperately searching for alternative forms of energy. The most common forms of renewable energy are nuclear, hydroelectric, solar, wind, and geothermal. All of these energy sources can be replaced in short order. However,

it should be noted that renewable sources of energy are not necessarily good for the environment. Nuclear energy has been responsible for many devastating natural disasters, and hydroelectric power systems manipulate the water system in potentially damaging ways.

Fossil fuel

Fossil fuels, so named because they are made of the decomposed bodies of prehistoric creatures, are a mixture of carbon and hydrogen molecules. Nevertheless, these fuels come in a number of different forms. Coal is a solid fossil fuel, made up primarily of carbon. It has to be extracted from the ground through mining. Natural gas, on the other hand, is a gas or liquid that has to be extracted from porous rocks. The main ingredient in natural gas is methane. Oil is a liquid fossil fuel that is found on or beneath the ground, either in large pools or soaked into porous rock. Oil is useless as fuel unless it is purified. Through the purification process, oil can be turned into kerosene, gasoline, and diesel fuel, among other products.

Potential energy

It is not easy to conceive of energy, in part because it comes in so many different forms. Wherever work is done, there is energy. Indeed, physics defines energy as the ability to do work. The unit of energy is the joule (J). Perhaps the most difficult form of energy to understand is potential energy (PE), the stored capacity for work in a physical body. For instance, when a brick is raised in the air, it acquires the potential energy to be pulled down by the gravitational force of the Earth. This particular form of potential energy is known as gravitational potential energy, and can be calculated by multiplying the object's mass by the force of gravity and the height to which the object has been raised. An object raised above the ground is storing energy to be used in a fall.

Kinetic energy

When an object is in motion, it has kinetic energy (KE). Kinetic energy is calculated by halving the mass of the object and multiplying it by the square of the object's velocity: $KE = \frac{1}{2}mv^2$. A heavy object will have more kinetic energy than a light one, and a fast object will have more kinetic energy than a slow one. Actually, the velocity of the object has much more effect on kinetic energy than the mass, as indicated by the fact that it is squared in the equation. A relatively small change in velocity can have a very large impact on the measure of kinetic energy.

Work

In physical science, work is defined as the energy required to exert a given force over a given distance. In fact, work is calculated by multiplying force by distance. The unit for work is the joule (J), also known as the newton-meter (N·m) because it combines the units for force and distance. One joule of work is performed when one newton of force is exerted over one meter. Note that unless there is motion, no work is performed. Pushing hard against a brick wall may feel like work, but it is not defined as such in physical science. Also, work requires that the force and distance be in the same direction. If the direction of the force is only part of the direction of the distance, then work can only be calculated for the component of distance moving in the same direction of the force. For instance, if you push a toy sailboat straight ahead but the wind carries it to the right at the same time, your work can only be figured for the distance the sailboat moves forward.

Power

Power is the measure of the amount of work performed in a certain interval. Another way of describing power is as the amount of energy changed in a given period. The basic equation for power is work divided by time. The unit of power is the joule per second, otherwise known as the watt (W). When one joule of work is performed in one second, one watt of power has been used. If, for example, a force of 10 N is required to move a book 1 meter, and the motion is accomplished in 2 seconds, the power is calculated 10N × 1m ÷ 2s = 5W. Note that power is inversely proportional to time; the faster work is done, the more power is used.

Work and power

When work is performed on an object, the kinetic energy of the object increases. Indeed, the change in the kinetic energy is equal to the amount of work performed. This is known as the work-energy theorem, and is expressed by the equation Work = ΔKE, where Δ (delta) means "the change in". This theorem can also be applied to decreases in kinetic energy: a heavy object moving quickly (that is, an object with a high level of kinetic energy) will require more work to be stopped. In addition, the work-energy theorem describes situations involving potential energy: when an object is lifted off the ground, the amount of work required to lift it is equal to the increase in its potential energy. Conversely, the gravitational force required to bring the object back to the ground is equal to the decrease, or negative change, in the object's potential energy.

Thermal energy

Thermal energy is the degree of motion of the atoms and molecules that make up a substance. Thermal energy is also referred to as heat, because the motion of atoms and molecules is related to the heat of the substance. Let's consider water as an example. As its thermal energy increases it moves from a solid (ice), to a liquid (water), and then to a gas (steam). Each change in state is accompanied by more movement by each individual water molecule. Likewise, your palms will produce more thermal energy (that is, they will get warmer) if you clap a few times. This is because the impact of the clapping actually causes the atoms in your skin to vibrate more.

Power from fossil fuels

The overwhelming majority of the Earth's energy is produced by burning fossil fuels. According to recent statistics, all but 16% of the energy consumed on Earth is produced by coal (22%), oil (37%), and natural gas (25%). Most fossil fuel-based power plants work according to a similar system. Fossil fuels are burned, and the resulting heat boils water and created steam. This steam is kept under high pressure and directed against the blades of a turbine. The whirling axis of the turbine is connected to a generator, where the kinetic motion of the blades is converted into electricity. The electricity generated is sent out from the power plant through a series of wires.

Solar and wind power

Although the sun provides more than enough energy to power the entire world, scientists have struggled to develop systems capable of harnessing this power. It was not until the 1990s that scientists established the first set of solar panels that stored energy as heat. This facility is in the Mojave Desert of California. At present, the solar cell is the most common way to convert the rays of the sun into electricity. Sunlight hits an outer layer of phosphorus and silicon, exciting electrons and generating current in a circuit. The current terminates in a layer of boron and silicon atoms. Wind power is also derived from the sun, specifically from the variations in temperature that create areas of low and high pressure, thus producing the shifts in air known as wind. The windmills of today are similar to those used hundreds of years ago: these days, the spinning blades power an electrical generator rather than a grinding wheel.

Hydroelectric and geothermal energy

Hydroelectric energy is generated from the flow of rapid rivers and streams. In a typical arrangement, a hydroelectric power plant is adjacent to a dam, which holds back a flowing body of water. Water from the resulting reservoir is directed through a series of channels (called penstocks) and used to spin large turbines. The rotation of the turbines powers an electrical generator. Geothermal energy, meanwhile, is obtained using the heat of the Earth. Specifically, geothermal power plants are based on extremely hot pools of subterranean water. A deep well is drilled into the pool, and the rising steam is used to spin turbines. Unfortunately, geothermal energy production is only practicable in areas where volcanic magma is close the surface, as for instance in New Zealand and California.

Nuclear energy

In nuclear power plants, scientists cause atoms to undergo nuclear fission (separation). The resulting chain reactions produce a great deal of energy, in the form of heat. This heat is applied to large pools of water, inside the familiar nuclear reactors. The steam rising off the water powers turbines, which are attached to electrical generators. The process of nuclear fission and nuclear energy creation is quite clean, but it requires the use of radioactive materials which are difficult to dispose of.

Scientists are optimistic that nuclear fusion will become a viable way of creating nuclear energy in the future. For the time being, however, concerns over the safety and environmental hazard of nuclear power generation limit its use.

Fuel cells

The most efficient way to convert chemical energy to electricity is with a fuel cell. In a hydrogen-oxygen fuel cell, there are separate reservoirs for the two gases. The hydrogen is oxidized and emits a number of electrons, which act as an electrical current flowing to the oxygen chamber. The oxygen is then reduced (that is, it gives up electrons), and the extra negative particles are carried back to the hydrogen chamber to begin the process anew. This flow of electrons throughout the fuel cell produces electricity and steam. Fuel cells have been used to power space shuttles and buildings, but engineers are still trying to develop small-scale models appropriate for cars. At present, the amount of hydrogen gas needed to power an automobile has too much volume to be functional.

Energy loss during conversion

Whenever energy is converted from one form to another, some of it is lost. Indeed, some fossil fuel power plants lose 2/3 of the energy they produce. The ways in which energy can be lost are several: burning fuels heat not only the water but the surrounding air and the water container; some steam escapes before it can power the turbines; the turbines are subject to friction forces; and some electricity escapes the generator cables. With the inevitability of energy loss in mind, scientists have set about developing ways to minimize inefficiencies. For instance, many countries use the water heated during electricity generation to warm homes in the winter or to use as bath water. This does not diminish energy loss, but rather gets more use out of the energy retained.

Energy conservation

One of the most amazing insights of physics is that the amount of energy in the universe never changes. This is known as the law of conservation of energy: energy cannot be created or destroyed; it can only be converted and transferred. When a brick falls to the ground, the kinetic energy of motion is transferred into the sound of the impact and the tiny amount of heat generated by the friction. When you eat a carrot, the chemical energy created by the sun is turned into cellular and muscular energy in your body, which in turn are expressed as motion. The overall amount of energy remains constant in every physical system. One of the challenges of technology is to ensure that as much energy as possible is applied to the intended task.

Energy efficiency

Efficiency is the degree to which a device uses the input energy to accomplish its intended task. Automobiles are relatively inefficient machines, because they use only about 20% of the energy from gasoline combustion to propel the car forward. The rest of the energy is lost through friction, wind resistance, heat loss, etc. Efficiency is equal to the amount of work done divided by the amount of energy consumed. It is usually expressed as a percentage; if 50 joules of work produce only 40 joules of energy towards our purpose, we are operating at only 80% efficiency. It is almost impossible to create a system that is totally efficient; friction forces and heat loss are constantly draining energy.

Electrical charge

An electrical charge is created when electrons are gained or lost. For instance, when you scuff your rubber-soled shoes on a carpet, you are transferring electrons from the carpet to your shoes. Then, when you touch the refrigerator, the charge you picked up from the carpet is transferred to the metal, giving you a little shock. The basic rule of electrical charge is that like charges repel and opposite charges attract. There are only two kinds of charge, positive and negative. Since electrons are negative, the object that gains electrons becomes negative and the object that loses electrons becomes positive. Note that no electrons are created or destroyed in the charging process. The resulting positive charge is equal to the negative charge, a phenomenon known as the conservation of charge.

Coulomb's law

Coulomb's law describes the force relationship between two charged particles. The formula for Coulomb's law is $F = k(q_1q_2/d^2)$, where F is force, k is a constant, q_1 is the charge of one particle, q_2 is the charge of the other particle, and d is the distance between the two particles. The distance between the particles is an inverse square of the force relationship, meaning that as the distance expands, the force between the particles decreases markedly. The proportionality constant k is similar to the force of gravity, insofar as it is consistent for all charged particles. One difference is that k can be either attractive or repulsive, while the force of gravity is always attractive. The unit of charge is the coulomb (C).

Electrical current

In a piece of metal, the electrons on the very outside of the atom are only loosely held together. Indeed, they can flow freely throughout the metal, enabling the conduction of heat and electrical energy. The flow of electrons is known as electrical current. The flow of electrons through a charged material is analogous to the flow of water. An electrical current only exists when there is a net flow of electrons in one direction. The random flow of electrons in all directions is typical of uncharged materials. Electrical current is measured in amperes (A). One ampere is equal to the rate of flow of one coulomb of charge per second.

Direct and alternating current

Direct current (dc) flows in one direction, while alternating current (ac) flows in one direction and then the other. The classic example of direct current is a battery system, in which the terminals of the battery always have the same charge, and the flow of electric current is from one to the other continuously. In a system with alternating current, on the other hand, the charges on the terminals of the generator (whether a battery or some other power source) are constantly switching back and forth. The electrons in an alternating system never really go anywhere; they simply quiver back and forth in place as the direction of the current shifts. Interestingly, even in a direct current system, electrons move at a speed of less than one centimeter per second.

Voltage

An electric current can only exist when there are more electrons in one area than another. The current is the result of electrons moving into areas of lower pressure, just as wind is the result of air moving from areas of high pressure to areas of low pressure. In an electrical system, pressure is known as voltage. The voltage of a system is directly proportional to the electric potential

- 54 -

energy of the system, a relationship that can be calculated as voltage = potential energy/charge. In other words, a higher voltage translates into a higher electrical potential energy. In order for voltage to exist, there must be a difference in pressure on opposing ends of the circuit. A battery is simply a device for creating this difference: one end of the battery generates high pressure, while the other generates low pressure. This ensures steady voltage.

Electrical resistance

The amount of electrical current in a circuit is dependent on the voltage and the resistance. Resistance is measured in ohms (Ω). The amount of resistance is influenced in part by the length and width of the wire. There is greater resistance in a longer and narrower wire. Like most features of electrical current, this is analogous to the flow of water: a long and narrow pipe will slow down water much more than a short, road pipe. The most important determinant of resistance, however, is the material through which the current must travel. Some metals, like copper, have almost no resistance, while rubber and other materials have an extremely high resistance. One way to decrease the resistance of a substance is to lower its temperature. When a material offers virtually no resistance, it is designated as a superconductor.

Ohm's law

The unit of electrical resistance, the ohm, is named for Georg Simon Ohm, a German scientist who explored electrical current, voltage, and resistance. He found that in a given circuit the current is directly proportional to the voltage and inversely proportional to the resistance. This relationship is known as Ohm's law, and as a formula is expressed current = voltage/resistance. It is common, however, to see Ohm's law written I = V/R, where I is current. In terms of units, the law is expressed amperes = volts/ohms. According to Ohm's law, the level of current will rise when the voltage rises, and by the same proportion. So, if current is doubled, voltage will be doubled as well. However, when current is doubled, resistance is halved.

Electric power

Electrical current is capable of doing work. The amount of work that a given current can do in an interval is called electric power. Electric power only exists when the current is converted into a different form of energy, as, for instance, when it is used to spin the blades of a fan or to light a bulb. Electric power, then, is the amount of transformed energy divided by the time elapsed. It is typically calculated by multiplying current by voltage. The unit of electric power is the watt (W). Many electrical devices and appliances list their power. For instance, power and voltage are printed on light bulbs. A light bulb with 60W of power and 120 V of voltage will require a current of 0.5 A.

Series and parallel circuits

In order to flow, electrons require a circuit, a complete and unbroken pathway. When a circuit contains more than one device powered by electrical energy, it is either arranged as a series circuit or a parallel circuit. In a series circuit, all of the devices are connected along the same pathway. For instance, in a simple series circuit a wire extends from a battery terminal to first one light bulb, then another light bulb, and finally to the other battery terminal. The path of the wire resembles a ring. The main problem with a series circuit is that the failure of one device breaks the entire circuit. In a parallel circuit, on the other hand, the wire extends out in branches to each device. Each device, then, has its own electron path.

Current in a series circuit

In a series circuit, the electric current only follows one path. For this reason, the current in a series circuit is the same in every part. The resistance in a series circuit is the sum of the resistances of all the devices. Assuming that there is no resistance in the wire, the total resistance can be derived by adding up the individual resistances of the devices. The current in a series circuit can be calculated by dividing the voltage of the source by the total resistance. Each device in a series circuit gets the same amount of voltage. Finally, the drop in voltage across each of the devices in a series circuit is in proportion to the resistance of the device. In other words, more energy is expended when the current must pass through a device with higher resistance.

Current in a parallel circuit

In a parallel circuit, each electric device is connected by a branch to the main part of the circuit. So, if one of the branches is broken, the rest of the circuit does not cease to work. In a parallel circuit, the flow of electricity, and therefore the voltage, is the same across every device. However, the total current in the circuit is divided up among the various branches, and so the more devices in the system, the lower the current in each branch. The quantity of current in each branch is inversely proportional to the resistance of the branch. Also, the current in the circuit is equal to the sum of the currents in all parallel branches. If more parallel branches are added, however, the resistance is lowered. In other words, the total resistance of the entire circuit is less than the resistance in any of the individual branches.

Electronic components

- Terminal: the point in a circuit where the current is either initiated or broken; for example, a battery has two terminals
- Resistor: controls the level of current in a circuit by providing resistance; in other words, voltage decreases as current passes through a circuit; most resistors work by converting electrical current into heat, which escapes into the air and is thus taken out of the system
- Diode: restricts the flow of current in one direction only; used to convert alternating current to direct current and to amplify the current in one direction; composed of two parts (anode and cathode)
- Amplifier: any device, such as a transistor or an electron tube, that increase the amplitude of an electrical current; in other words, an amplifier receives an input signal and produces a larger signal with an identical wave form
- Capacitor: (also known as a condenser) stores electrical charge temporarily; typically composed of two metal plates separated by a thin insulator (often air); used for controlling and moderating current
- Transducer: converts energy into a different form; for instance, a microphone converts sound energy into electricity, a photoelectric cell converts light energy into electricity, and a loudspeaker converts electricity into sound
- Detector: identifies and possibly responds to certain electrical signals

- Transistor: can function in a circuit as a detector, switch, or amplifier

Electronic devices

- Transformer: shifts electric energy from one circuit to another, often with a change in current or voltage; for example, a small transformer is used to diminish the current flowing through a doorbell, in order to reduce the risk of serious shock
- Switch: alternately completes, diverts, or breaks a circuit
- Relay: a type of switch that, when activated by a small current, initiates a larger current; when the small current reaches the relay, a gate is closed, thus completing the circuit for the larger current; relays are used in television and telephone transmission, in which a small input signal initiates the broadcast of a much larger signal

Internal combustion motors

An internal combustion motor converts chemical energy into mechanical energy through burning. Motors are referred to as internal combustion when the burning takes place on the inside. The fuel combusts in small cylinders inside the motor. Each cylinder contains a piston, which is driven up and down by the tiny combustions of fuel. These up-and-down movements turn a crankshaft, which in a car is used to rotate the wheels. Some internal combustion motors have carburetors, which vaporize gasoline before it enters the cylinders, while others have fuel injectors, which inject gasoline vapor into the cylinder after it has been filled with compressed air. One of the problems with internal combustion

motors is that they lose much of their energy in the form of heat.

Electrical motors

Electric motors convert magnetic force into kinetic energy. In a direct current (DC) motor, a wire coil is placed in between two pieces of charged metal. A current running through the coil gives it a magnetic charge and causes it to rotate. The end of the coil can be attached to a shaft and used to do work. For instance, the coil could be connected to the axis of a fan blade, so that when it spins the blades rotate as well. There are a couple of devices used to refine the operation of an electric motor. A commutator reverses the charge of the wire every time it makes a half-rotation. This ensures the continuous spinning of the wire, since every time the positive side of the coil approaches the negative piece of metal, its charge is reversed and it must continue spinning to reach the positively charged metal.

Cams, gears, and linkages

- Cams: an elliptical wheel that, when connected to a driveshaft, powers some mechanical motion; in an automobile engine, for instance, the up-and-down motion of the pistons rotates the cams, causing the wheels to move forward
- Gears: interlocking toothed wheels, one of which is connected to a shaft; when the shaft is twisted, the drive wheel spins in one direction and causes the other wheel to be spun in the opposite direction; if the other wheel is smaller than the drive wheel, it spins more quickly but produces less force; if the other wheel is larger than the drive wheel, it

moves more slowly but produces a greater force

- Linkages: a system of connected bars held together by springs or hinges; the piston, rod, and crank in a car engine comprise a four-bar linkage

Pneumatics and hydraulics

Pneumatic systems operate with the aid of compressed air. Pneumatic systems are known for being safe, because compressed air is not flammable. Hydraulic systems, on the other hand, rely on the pressure exerted by liquid in a tube. In an automotive brake system, for instance, pulling the handle presses fluid against a lever that in turn forces the brake pad against the tire rim. Hydraulic systems work because most liquids cannot be compressed. Hydraulic systems are known for being efficient, and for being able to generate more force than pneumatics.

Pulleys and transmissions

- Pulley: a simple machine composed of at least one wheel with a rope extended around the rim, such that the wheel spins when the rope is pulled; the use of pulley systems can create great mechanical advantage (energy output is much greater than energy input); for instance, a two-pulley system is capable of halving the energy required to lift an object off of the ground
- Transmission: the component of a machine that directs the energy created to the intended task; for instance, an automotive transmission takes the spinning of the crankshaft and coverts it into the mechanical work of turning the axle

Basic motor maintenance and repair

The better part of motor maintenance is regular cleaning and oiling. Mechanics are able to keep engines running for decades so long as they are periodically lubricated and tested. Lubrication minimizes the friction in the engine, and keeps heat and abrasion from destroying the components. Most mechanics recommend replacing certain parts (as for instance the drive belts in an automotive engine) every so often in order to prevent more serious and expensive problems. In recent years, many car and other engines have been outfitted with computer systems to monitor performance. Mechanics must be able to evaluate data as well as perform the necessary repairs.

Transportation

Transportation planners address transportation issues at both the local and regional levels. They research different modes of transportation (automobiles, bicycles, ride-sharing, etc.), forecast the impact of those modes using computer modeling, and promote alternative transportation modes. Transportation planning usually requires a two-year degree in transportation technology.

Transit operations analysts examine mass transit operations, such as trains and buses, and determine how they can better serve the community through either new technologies or revised procedures. This career normally requires a two-year degree in transportation technology.

Civil Engineering Technicians assist in the planing, design and construction of transportation structures such as highways, subways, railways, tunnels and airports. They analyze highway survey data and traffic signal timing, conduct repair work on damaged structures, and collaborate with CAD technicians to create maps and building specifications. Civil Engineering Technicians usually require a two-year degree in civil engineering and can work in a variety of organizations, both public and private.

Rail, air and road

Rail transportation is the use of a railway, which is simply either a set of two steel rails running parallel and connected by ties; a monorail, which is a single rail; or a maglev, which is magnetic suspension. A train runs along the railway, and can be powered in a variety of ways including steam, diesel, electricity, gas turbines, gravity, cables, and others.

Air transportation is the use of aircraft (such as airplanes, helicopters and gyroplanes) to reach a destination. Aircraft will not operate properly without air flow to provide lift and an area reserved for landing. The air transportation industry makes use of airports for loading, maintenance, and refueling. Air transportation is one of the fastest modes of transportation.

Road transportation is the use of prepared pathways (paved, smoothed, etc.) to travel between multiple places. A prominent example is a highway. Roads are most commonly used by automobiles, such as cars, buses and trucks. Bicycles and pedestrians also make use of the road system. Although automobiles are very adaptable, they have poor energy efficiency and create pollution.

Marine, space, and intermodal

Marine transportation is the use of boats, ships, barges and other buoyant transports that utilize water. Marine craft use a variety of propulsion methods such as wind power, steam power, petroleum engines and nuclear energy. Marine transport is highly efficient and cost effective, but tends to be slow. Its

primary commercial use is transportation of non-perishable goods.

Space transport is the use of spacecraft to travel into space. Examples include space shuttles, satellites, and rockets. It is the rarest form of transportation.

Intermodal transportation is the use of multiple transportation systems to reach a destination. For instance, if a person orders a piece of furniture online, it may be transported on an airplane and a truck before it reaches its destination.

Problems associated with transportation systems

Transportation systems have greatly enhanced mankind's ability to travel and opened up new possibilities for both work and recreation. However, advances in transportation have not come without problems. For instance, as the population within cities increases, the number of cars and motorists increases as well. This creates problems such as traffic congestion and air pollution, especially within heavily urbanized areas. A possible solution is better public transportation systems, such as monorails, buses and subway systems. Another solution is to build residences nearer to places of work so that people have the option of walking or biking to their jobs. Another problem with transportation systems is urban sprawl, which occurs when people live outside the city and then commute in for work. Urban sprawl not only increases air pollution, it requires removal of natural habitats, further displacing animal populations and limiting their food supply.

Internal combustion engine and external combustion engine

An internal combustion engine, or ICE, generates propulsive force through the combustion of fuel—usually gasoline or a similar energy-dense liquid—and air within a combustion chamber. This action produces high pressure gas that is directed over a piston, turbine, nozzle, or similar engine component. ICEs serve as the primary means of power generation in all types of automobiles, aircraft, and water transports. Common types of ICEs include two-stroke engines, four-stroke engines, diesel engines, wankel engines, jet engines and gas turbines.

An external combustion engine, or ECE, generates propulsive force by using an external heat source to heat and cause expansion in a fluid. The heat sources acts through a heat exchanger or engine wall. The fluid is then cooled and reused. Common types of ECEs include steam engines and Stirling engines.

Transportation industries

The automotive industry performs functions related to the design, creation, manufacturing and marketing of automobiles. Many automobile manufacturers in the United States are part of a trade group known as The Alliance of Automobile Manufacturers, which represents their common interests and works to fulfill social transportation needs.

The automotive repair and service industry handles repairs and servicing of automobiles after they have been purchased by the consumer. The National Institute for Automotive Service Excellence, or ASE, provides training and certification to service technicians and professionals in the United States.

The airline industry transports passengers and cargo via air transportation. There are commercial airlines in most of the civilized world. To become a commercial aircraft service in the United States, an aircraft operator

must be granted an air operator's certificate (AOC) by the National Aviation Authority, or NAA.

The shipping industry transports passengers and cargo via water transportation. It serves commercial, recreational and military purposes, and is less expensive than air travel.

Fossil fuels, steam, electricity and gravity

Fossil fuels are created from decomposition of dead animals and plants over a period of time. Fossil fuels such as petroleum are especially important in transportation because they provide a variety of fuels, such as gasoline, diesel fuel, oil, and jet fuel. Fossil fuels are considered non-renewable resources because their current rate of usage exceeds their rate of renewal.

Steam is created by boiling water, and then harnessed to power steam engines, which propel transports such as locomotives, tractors, and ships. Fossil fuels, solar energy, nuclear energy, and geothermal energy often provide the heat necessary to create steam.

Electricity is often used to power trains and street cars via electric lines. It can also increase the efficiency or serve as the sole power source of a car engine.

Gravity is used to power rail systems.

Buoyancy and gravitational acceleration

Buoyancy is a force that causes objects to float in a fluid, such as air or water. Buoyancy is generated because there is more pressure at the bottom of a column of fluid than the top; consequently, objects that are less dense than the fluid rise to the top while denser objects sink. In air transportation, buoyancy is a key consideration in lighter-than-air modes of transport, such as hot air balloons and blimps. The gas within the balloon or blimp will only be pushed up (i.e. float) if it less dense than the surrounding air. In marine transportation, ships hulls must be designed such that they are less dense than the surrounding water; otherwise, they will not float.

Gravitational acceleration is a downward force exerted on an object by gravity. It is used as the primary means of propulsion for certain types of rail systems. In the absence of friction, all objects fall at the same rate. In the presence of air friction, buoyancy will cause denser objects to fall faster.

Momentum, inertia, and weight

Momentum equals an object's mass multiplied by its velocity ($p = mv$), and indicates both the direction and magnitude of an object. When objects collide, they transfer their momentum to each other. Momentum helps engineers predict and determine the outcome of a collision between two objects.

Inertia is an object's innate resistance to changes in its state of motion or rest. Put simply, a stationary object will remain stationary and a moving object will remain moving unless they are acted upon by outside forces. More massive objects possess more inertia than less massive ones. Inertia helps designers to understand the level of force necessary to propel a particular mode of transport.

Weight is a force that gravity applies on an object. An object will not fly unless its thrust-to-weight ratio is greater than the pull of gravity. An object's weight will vary according to the strength of the gravitational field in which it is situated.

Propulsion, energy storage and guidance

Propulsion is achieved through the following means:
- Air transportation – generates thrust by pushing airflow over a wing.
- Marine transportation – relies on propellers driven by some type of internal combustion or steam engine. Some ships still rely on oars or sails.
- Space transportation – uses a rocket engine to expel hot gas.
- Road and rail transportation – relies on wheels driven by some type of power force (e.g., combustion engines, electric motors, animal muscle).

Energy storage is the process of using devices or media to store energy for use at a later time. For instance, batteries and fuel cells can store electrical energy for use in electric motors. Petroleum and other fossil fuels store energy for use in internal combustion engines.

Guidance is the process of controlling the movement, speed and navigation of craft. In air transportation, guidance is achieved through manipulating ailerons, rudders, fuel pumps, and similar devices. In marine transportation, it is achieved by adjusting sails or manipulating rudders. In road transportation, it is normally achieved through a steering mechanism.

Vehicle tracking and dispatch

Dispatch is a vehicle assignment procedure used by companies that operate fleets of vehicles. A dispatcher receives call information from customers, and then assigns a vehicle to the customer based on the order in which the call was received and the proximity of the driver to the customer's location. Computer assisted dispatch increases the efficiency of the dispatch procedure by using various software applications and devices, such as GPS. In some systems, each truck may record information through an onboard GPS system. This information is downloaded once the truck returns to its base. In other systems, the truck may be able to communicate and relay its position in real time to the base. The latter system is more expensive but enhances efficiency.

Vehicle tracking is a system capable of determining the location, speed, and direction of a fleet vehicle. The system can be based on GPS or satellite tracking technology.

Thrust, lift, and drag

Thrust is a reaction force that occurs when mass expelled or accelerated in one direction causes a proportional force in the opposite direction. In air transportation, thrust is generated by pushing airflow over a wing, usually by means of a spinning propeller, a fan pulling air through a jet engine, or a rocket engine expelling hot gas. In marine transportation, propellers generate thrust by accelerating water in one direction.

Drag is a force created by a fluid (such as air or water) passing over an object. Drag exerts a force that runs parallel to and opposes the movement of an oncoming object.

Lift is a surface force created by a fluid (such as air or water) passing over an object. Lift exerts a force that goes perpendicular to the direction of an oncoming object. In air transportation, airfoils must generate sufficient thrust and lift to overcome drag; otherwise, the object will not fly. Lift is not limited to upward movement. By adjusting the

shape of a wing, aircraft can generate the lift required to climb, descend or bank.

Fleet management, driver training, fleet expenditure management, routing and scheduling

Fleet management seeks to decrease the risks, improve the productivity and lower the operating costs of a company's fleet of vehicles. Fleet management encompasses many different functions, such as vehicle tracking, diagnostics, maintenance, fuel usage, and health and safety.
Driver training should include courses on performing basic vehicle maintenance, improving driver skills, and following certain procedures when the driver is involved in an accident.

Fleet expenditure management should include a system for account management, handling tax invoices electronically, and fuel management.

Routing involves selecting the paths and roadways a group of vehicles will use to reach their destinations. Selections will be made based on the roads which provide the most efficient and effective means of access.

Scheduling is the process of assigning customers to routes. The goal is to optimize the efficiency with which drivers can service customers.

Pneumatics and hydraulics

Pneumatics is a type of fluid power that creates mechanical movement through the use of pressurized gas, such as compressed air. In transportation, pneumatics has a variety of applications:
- Air brakes on buses, trucks, and trains.
- Air engines, pneumatic motors, and compressed air engines in locomotives, automobiles, and

commercial airlines which use compressed air to start their main engines.

- Pneumatic tires, which are filled with compressed air.

Hydraulics is a type of fluid power that creates mechanical movement through the use of incompressible liquids. These liquids are pressurized and then used to transmit power throughout the system. In transportation, hydraulic principles are often incorporated into brakes. Hydraulic systems use far higher pressures than pneumatic systems, can generate much greater forces and can bear much greater loads, and consist of the following components: hydraulic pumps, control valves, actuators, accumulators, filters, and hydraulic fluids.

Transmission and gear

A transmission, also known as a gearbox, uses gear ratios to convert between speed and torque. In an automobile, the transmission receives output from the internal combustion engine via the crankshaft, and then transmits power to differentials (drive wheels) via the drive shaft. Transmissions are necessary because the engine operates at a much higher RPM (revolutions per minute) than the wheels rotate. The transmission converts speed into torque at lower velocities and then torque into speed at higher velocities, such as highway driving. Transmissions can also increase fuel efficiency.

A gear is a circular rotating component with cogs cut into it around the edges. These cogs mesh with the cogs of another gear, and thereby transmit torque (i.e. rotational force) between the gears. A transmission is simply two or more meshed gears working together. The gear ratio is the relative number of cogs between two meshed gears. When a

smaller cog is turning a larger cog, the larger cog possesses more torque.

Pistons and crank shaft

A piston converts pressure into rotational force. It is a reciprocating component inside an internal combustion engine as well as other types of reciprocating engines. The piston is contained within a cylinder. When gas expands inside the cylinder, the piston is driven down and up in a continuous reciprocating motion, which is transmitted to the crankshaft through piston rods or connecting rods.

A crankshaft converts linear motion of the pistons into rotational motion that passes through the transmission and eventually turns the wheels. The crankshaft is connected to the pistons via a series of rods. Each rod is connected to a crank pin—a section of the crankshaft with an axis that does not line up exactly with the main axis of the crankshaft. By pushing down on these pins, the linear force is converted into rotational force.

Belt and pulley system

A belt and pulley system consists of multiple pulleys connected to a belt. A pulley is a wheel that is part of an axle or shaft, and is also known as a drum or a sheave. In some cases, the belt may fit into a groove running around the circumference of the wheel. When the belt is pulled, it transmits torque and speed over the axles to which it is connected. A belt and pulley system can perform speed and torque conversions if the pulleys differ in size. The ratio between the sizes determines the nature of the conversion. There are three types of pulley systems: A fixed or class 1 system has a fixed axle and a mechanical advantage of 1, meaning the force is not multiplied. A movable or class 2 system has a free axle that can move in space, and applies a mechanical advantage of 2,

- 63 -

meaning the force is doubled on the object attached to the pulley. A compound pulley incorporates class 1 and class 2 systems. A block and tackle is a type of compound pulley in which each axle has several pulleys.

Weak compression within an internal combustion engine

Weak compression within an internal combustion engine can have a variety of causes, and there are simple methods for determining these causes:

- If a compression test shows that one cylinder has low compression, put a small amount of oil into the cylinder. Test its compression again. If the compression reads normally, then the engine simply has worn piston rings. If the compression does not increase, the engine may have leaky valves or a blown head gasket. If compression increases but does not return to normal, the engine may have worn piston rings and leaky valves.
- When two neighboring cylinders have low compression, the engine likely has a leaking head gasket. Adjust the head bolts so they match engine specifications. Retest the compression. If the compression does not return to normal, remove the head gasket and examine the engine blocks for cracks. If no cracks are discovered, replace the head gasket.

Testing compression

A compression test checks the compression within each cylinder of an internal combustion engine. The test requires a compression gauge, and follows these basic steps:

1. Ensure the battery is completely charged and the automobile's tuning is good. Take the car on a 20 minute drive so that all engine components have reached full operating temperature.
2. Determine appropriate engine compression and operating parameters by consulting a shop manual.
3. Ensure that the engine is turned off. Remove all spark plugs and disconnect the ignition coil. This prevents the engine from starting. Block open the throttle and choke.
4. Crank the engine as you test the compression. Insert the compression gauge into each engine cylinder, and record the reading. Reset gauge back to 0 before moving on to the next cylinder.
5. Determine if there are any pressure differences between cylinders, and compare all cylinders against operating specifications. If the differences are too great, the engine may have a problem.

Vacuum test

A vacuum test is performed with a pressure gauge, which is also known as a vacuum gauge. It measures the difference between the air pressure inside and outside of the intake manifold. A vacuum test can find intake manifold gasket leaks, ignition issues, blocked exhaust systems, burned valves, weak springs, and other problems. It follows these basic steps:

1. Ensure that the battery is completely charged and that the automobile's tuning is good. Take the car on a 20 minute drive so all engine components have reached full operating temperature.
2. Attach the vacuum gauge. On a car, fasten the vacuum gauge where the vacuum tubing leads to

the windshield wiper motor. If necessary, detach the vacuum booster pump on the windshield wiper. This may interfere with the accuracy of the readings. Ensure that all connections are airtight.

3. Turn on the engine and allow it to idle. A healthy, well-tuned engine will idle at a reading between 18 and 22 inches at sea level. Large fluctuations in the reading or a lower reading than expected indicate an engine problem.

Weak or fluctuating vacuum readings

If a vacuum test on an internal combustion engine produces large fluctuations in readings, it indicates a problem with some (but not all) of the cylinders. Possible problems include the following:

- Intake manifold leak in one cylinder.
- Wear in the intake valve guides.
- Defective piston or piston rings.
- Faulty throttle shaft.

If a vacuum test produces low but constant readings, it indicates a problem with all cylinders. Possible problems include the following:

- Poor value timing.
- Faulty vacuum lines.
- Faulty carburetor throttle shaft.
- Damaged flange gasket.

By revving the engine to 2000 RPM and repeating the vacuum test, a tester can check for additional problems, such as ignition, timing, sticking valves, manifold leaks, and an incorrect mixture.

Creating automobile engines, ships' hulls and airplanes

Engine blocks for automobiles are typically made of cast iron; however, the reciprocating pistons within the engine generally consist of aluminum. As the engine warms up, the aluminum cylinders will begin expanding into their cast cylinder bores. The bores must be large enough to accommodate the pistons when the engine is hot; consequently, the bores will be very loose when the engine is cold. Compression tests should only be conducted when the engine is hot.

Modern ships' hulls are made of steel with various structural members, such as bulkheads, girders, and stringers. Hulls must be watertight and mostly hollow so that the ship has enough buoyancy to float.

Commercial airplanes are built using aluminum alloys and composite materials. Titanium is used in constructing both the jet's engine as well as other structural members.

Biotechnology and Computer Technology

Careers

The field of biotechnology is broad and lucrative. In addition, research continues to develop new areas for study, so the job supply is ever increasing. Perhaps the most basic job in biotechnology is the lab technician. Lab techs are employed by police departments, research facilities, and medical institutions. A quality control analyst is a special employee who continuously monitors lab performance to ensure that standards are being met. A bioinformatician uses computer science skills to convert the data gathered through research to actionable information. A biomedical engineer builds the equipment and develops the materials that make biotechnological research possible. Finally, a validation technician ensures that research adheres to the law and to the rules established by regulatory agencies and professional organizations. These professionals also work to improve productivity and efficiency within the lab.

Anthropometrics and ergonomics

Anthropometrics is a systematic approach to measuring the human body. It originated after the Second World War, as designers began to notice that many machines and pieces of furniture were inappropriately configured for human bodies. It became clear that designing better-sized machines could improve productivity as well as comfort. At around the same time, the field of ergonomics was exploring how better design could reduce injury in the workplace. Ergonomically inclined designers used the data generated through anthropometrics to create equipment that was easier to use and less taxing on the body. An emphasis on ergonomics was enshrined in United States law by the Occupational Health and Safety Act, which established some conditions for workplace furniture and equipment.

Joint replacements and prosthetics

Advances in medical technology have made joint and limb replacement surgery an increasingly viable option for victims of pain or dysfunction. The most common joints to be replaced are the knees and hips. Typically, a hip replacement will entail replacing both the hip socket and the top of the femur; this leg bone will be cut off at the top so that the replacement bone and socket can be attached. An artificial limb, known as a prosthesis, must be precisely measured so that it will not throw off the balance of the body. Laser measurement techniques have made it possible to calculate the appropriate length for a prosthesis within thousandths of an inch. There are prosthetics available for every limb of the body, though the most common are arms and legs below the knee. There are now electronic prostheses that respond to nerve impulses and actually perform the movements of the limb they have replaced. For instance, there are amazing prosthetic arms capable of grasping and lifting objects in response to the myoelectric impulses transmitted by the muscles of the upper arm to which it is attached.

Artificial organs

Biomedical research has produced artificial replacements for virtually every organ of the human body. There are electronic devices that stimulate certain parts of the brain, providing relief from depression and epilepsy. There are artificial ears that actually enable the recipient to hear. Artificial eyes are still improving, but already they have restored sight to many blind people. The most popular artificial organ is the replacement kidney. It functions like a dialysis unit, passing blood through a solution that extracts waste matter and restores electrolytes. Artificial bladders are unique in that they have been grown from living tissue in the laboratory. Artificial pancreases incorporate living tissue into a donor pancreas, which minimizes the risk of rejection by the recipient's body. Stem cell research has enabled doctors to grow replacement organs with cells from the recipient's own body. Perhaps the most difficult organ to replicate has been the heart. As of yet, there is not an artificial heart capable of sustaining life for more than a year and a half, though even this is quite a feat.

Common devices for monitoring health

A blood glucose meter helps people with diabetes keep track of their blood sugar levels. These devices are portable and easy to use. The most common version uses a small tack to draw a tiny blood sample, though there are also devices that measure blood sugar in the urine. A sphygmomanometer measures blood pressure. Inexpensive versions of this device are now available for personal use. In addition, there are now personal cholesterol monitors that let people keep track of their levels of triglycerides, cholesterol (including HDL), glucose, and ketones. These devices are valuable for people with heart problems. Digital thermometers are ubiquitous, and can provide a much more accurate measure of body temperature than mercury thermometers. Finally, there are a wide array of electronic asthma devices, including nebulizers (inhaler), spirometers (measures lung capacity), and peak flow meters.

Orthotics

Orthotics is the branch of medicine related to creating devices that improve physical performance and reduce pain. An orthosis, commonly called a brace, may control movement, limit the range of motion, provide support, or reduce the ability to bear weight on a certain part of the body. A common example of an orthosis is a back brace, which may be specially designed to treat a problem like lordosis or may simply diffuse the weight borne by the spine. The introduction of computer measurement has made it possible to create personalized braces quite inexpensively. Also, the development of extremely hard and durable plastics has enabled the production of lightweight, long-lasting braces. These devices have helped remediate pain and speed rehabilitation for millions of people.

Reproducing DNA in a laboratory through polymerase chain reaction

Scientists have developed a technique, called polymerase chain reaction, for reproducing segments of DNA. Living cells are not required for this process. In a matter of hours, it is possible to create 100 billion molecules that are exactly the same as a given DNA molecule. This process can be used in DNA fingerprinting, molecular biology, and biomedical technology. The process is complex, but it basically entails separating the two strands of the DNA double helix, isolating a section of the DNA to be replicated, and then using an enzyme to catalyze the formation of new bonds in that section. The result is that the amount of DNA in the specimen is doubled. Every time the process is repeated, the amount of DNA is doubled, so the total amount of DNA quickly gets very large.

DNA technology in criminal science

The development of effective DNA identification procedures has revolutionized the branch of criminal science known as forensics. If doctors and law enforcement officers are able to recover some fresh tissue, blood, or semen after a violent crime, they can identify the perpetrator beyond a shadow of doubt. To begin with, laboratory technicians will use antibodies to identify the surface cells of the sample, which will indicate the particular type of tissue or fluid. Then, the DNA will be isolated and special enzymes will be applied to it. These enzymes cut the DNA into fragments. The fragments are different for every person, though identical twins will have the same fragmentation patterns. By analyzing the pattern of fragments, forensic scientists can make conclusive matches between samples taken from a crime scene and samples taken from suspects.

Improving air quality

Scientists have developed a number of ways to use microorganisms in the improvement of air quality. For instance, biofiltering is a technique in which microbes are placed on a support medium, like a sheet of plastic, and then bathed with aqueous nutrients. The microbes extract contaminants from a gas. In some instances, biofilters have removed 90 percent of the contamination. A similar method, bioscrubbing, entails the introduction of a microbe-filled liquid to the contaminated gas. This technique has also proved successful, though it can be difficult to enact on a small scale. Some labs have found it difficult to manage the pH of the resulting gas, while others have complained that the bioscrubber has an unpleasant smell. For these reasons, biotechnological efforts at air quality improvement have not been readily adopted by industry.

Resolving oil spills

There are several methods for cleaning up oil spills. One is bioremediation, in which microbes that "eat" oil are introduced in large quantities to the spill site. Another common approach for spills in water is to burn the surface oil carefully off. In some cases, oily water will be sucked up into a centrifuge, where it can be spun rapidly until the oil separates from the water. Oil may be skimmed off the water surface. Another approach is to add dry hydrophobic solidifiers, which mix with the oil and form a solid that can be more easily removed. Finally, scientists have developed dispersant (or detergent) chemicals that adhere to oil globules, neutralize them, and allow them to wash away naturally without damaging the environment.

Desalinization

When the salt content of soil becomes too high, a process known as salinization, it can prevent plant growth. Excessive salinization can effectively turn arable land into a desert. Areas that are frequently irrigated are susceptible to this problem, because even fresh water contains a tiny amount of salt. Irrigation washes away soluble nutrients and leaves behind a salt precipitate. This phenomenon suggests the need for a technique of soil desalinization. At the same time, converting salt water from the ocean into drinking water requires desalinization. Thus, scientists have spent a great deal of time trying to develop an efficient means of removing salt from soil and water. The easiest way to remove salt from water is to heat the water within a glass or plastic enclosure, so that the salt adheres to the outside and can be scraped away. However, this typically requires a great deal of heating fuel.

Bioremediation

In bioremediation, microbes convert hazardous waste into other, less harmful materials. This process can be executed at the site of waste production or disposal. The most successful cases of bioremediation involve the use of microbes that already exist in the hazardous substance. For instance, many polychlorinated biphenyls and pesticides contain natural microbes that can be used in bioremediation. In addition, many laboratories are at work on genetically modified microbes that perform the same task. Some microbes are even capable of removing the toxins from heavy metals. Bioremediation is lauded by environmentalists and the general public, but it is unfortunately also very expensive, and therefore not used as often as it could be. Most companies determine that it is more cost-effective to bury their hazardous waste. Nevertheless, bioremediation has generated hope for future improvements in hazardous waste disposal.

Biostimulation and hazardous waste

Scientists are constantly working on techniques for accelerating the removal of hazardous waste from the environment. One such technique is biostimulation, in which nitrogen-rich compounds are added to microbes in the hopes of speeding up natural bioremediation. Contaminated water sources have been improved rapidly by infusions of methane, which promotes the growth of local bacteria that clean the water. Another method of improving bioremediation is to increase the accessibility, or bioavailability, of insoluble toxins to remediating plants and microbes. Scientists must be careful when increasing bioavailability, because a toxic substance that is more accessible to microbes is also more accessible to other organisms. It is important to combine these efforts with measures to prevent the toxins from entering the soil. The bioavailability of some hazardous wastes has been increased by heating, moistening, and treating with surfactants.

Wood pellets and methane production

The invention and popularization of wood pellets have created a new way for people to obtain energy from the combustion of wood. Flammable wood is compressed into tiny pellets, which are burned in a special stove. These stoves are equipped with electronic sensors that automatically load more pellets when necessary to maintain a target temperature. These wood pellet stoves are extremely efficient and require very little care during their operation. Another source of energy from biogas is through the production of methane. When sewage undergoes anaerobic digestion, it produces a biogas that is mostly methane. The remaining components of the biogas can be used as fertilizer. Many rural and poor areas have developed systems for converting waste into fuel and fertilizer. In a typical setup, waste matter is placed in a well, where it is mixed with an equal amount of water and allowed to sit until the digestion process is complete. The methane can then be used for heating and cooking, while the fertilizer is great for agriculture.

Ethanol and biodiesel

Ethanol is a popular alternative fuel created by fermenting starches or sugars, most commonly corn or sugar cane. The resulting alcohol is distilled so that it can be used to power vehicles. At present, the cost of producing ethanol makes it much more expensive than gasoline, so ethanol is typically mixed with regular gas to make "gasohol." In countries like Brazil, there is a thriving ethanol industry. Ethanol makes fuel burn cleaner. In the United States, it is especially popular in the Midwest, because it provides an outlet for excess corn. Another alternative fuel, biodiesel, is made from vegetable oil. In most cases, biodiesel consists of 20% natural oil and 80% regular diesel fuel. Many biodiesel manufacturers obtain their oil from the deep fryers of local restaurants. Like ethanol, biodiesel is better for the environment than regular gasoline. However, it is also costly to manufacture, and only works in diesel engines.

Applications of bioengineering to medicine

One of the earliest examples of bioengineering in medicine is amniocentesis, a technique for identifying chromosomal abnormalities in fetuses. In recent years, DNA probes have made it possible to isolate individual sequences of DNA and thereby learn about mutations in the genes. This would enable doctors to identify problems with fetuses conceived through in vitro fertilization. Some of the most common medical products of bioengineering are based on recombinant DNA technology, which encourages the creation of specific proteins. The most popular recombinant DNA products are insulin, interferons, and erythropoietins. Interferons fight specific diseases, while erythropoietins encourage the production of red blood cells. Recombinant DNA is most often produced in bacterial cells, though yeast and mammalian cells are also used for certain applications. Scientists are very optimistic about the possibility of creating recombinant DNA in egg whites. Similar technology has been used to create transgenic varieties of corn, potatoes, and tobacco.

Dialysis

Dialysis is a medical procedure for failing kidneys. When a person's kidneys stop working, a dangerous level of toxins can build up in the body. One way to resolve this is to process the blood outside of the body. In dialysis, the blood is taken out of the body and passed through a special machine that filters out the toxins. A dialysis machine has a selectively permeable membrane that functions like the nephrons at the end of tubules inside the kidneys. This membrane allows urea and salts to pass out of the blood, while glucose passes in the other direction and reenters the stream. The blood then leaves the machine and is fed back into the person's body. Dialysis is an effective technique, but it takes several hours and must be performed three times a week. For this reason, many people with failing kidneys prefer to receive a kidney transplant if possible.

Laser surgery

In laser surgery, a concentrated beam of light severs tissue precisely and cleanly. Lasers may be used to perform the cuts normally made with a scalpel, or may be used to vaporize extremely moist flesh. Perhaps the most widely known form of laser surgery is the LASIK eye procedure, in which a laser cuts the cornea and corrects near- or far-sightedness. One advantage of laser surgery is that no physical contact is required, so there is very little risk of infection. Also, computer-guided lasers are able to make much more precise and even cuts than even the finest human hand. The scars from laser surgeries heal more quickly and with considerably less pain. Indeed, lasers have even been used at low intensity levels to encourage wound healing.

Pacemakers and defibrillators

An artificial pacemaker is an electronic device that provides the rhythmic electrical impulses necessary for proper heart function. When a person's natural pacemaker is degraded or destroyed, doctors can implant a tiny electrode attached to a small generator to replicate its function. A temporary pacemaker may be affixed to the outside of the chest, while a permanent one may be attached to the heart itself. A somewhat similar device is the electronic defibrillator, which delivers a sharp electrical shock to the heart in the event of arrhythmia and cardiac arrest. A typical defibrillator consists of two pads attached by wires to a generator. The pads are placed on the chest and the generator sends a series of increasingly powerful charges to the heart, with the intention of restoring a normal natural rhythm.

Yeast

Yeast is a microscopic fungus that brewers and bakers have used for millennia in food production. Yeast, when deprived of oxygen, will ferment sugar and other substances. Fermentation creates adenosine triphosphate without requiring oxygen. When yeast ferments something, ethyl alcohol and carbon dioxide are produced. In the brewing process, the fermentation caused by yeast makes beer bubbly and intoxicating. In bread, the release of carbon dioxide causes the dough to expand during the baking process. The heat of baking evaporates the ethyl alcohol created by fermentation, which is why bread is not alcoholic. In both brewing and baking, yeast ferments because it is mixed with other substances such that it is no longer exposed to oxygen. Yeast will not ferment if it is simply placed on top of bread dough, however.

Industrial use of bioreagents

A bioreagent is a chemical that is extracted from a living cell and used as a reagent during some production process. Bioreagents are currently used in the production of pharmaceuticals, food, chemicals, and textiles. For instance, pharmaceutical steroids are made from plant steroids using bioreagents. Other cellular enzymes are used in the production of high-fructose corn syrup, a popular sweetener in processed foods. To find the right bioreagent for a particular process, a company first has to find a cell that is already performing the desired task. Then, the company must examine the amino acid sequences of each enzyme in the cell until it can be determined which enzyme is responsible. Another method for finding the right bioreagent is to isolate the mRNA in a cell that is performing the desired process and see into which enzymes that mRNA translates. A final method is to assemble collections of inactive cells, add promising enzymes, and see which cells begin to behave in the desired manner.

Hydroponics

Hydroponics is a system for growing plants by placing their roots in an inorganic salt solution rather than soil. This technique was pioneered in the eighteenth century, and was the first to suggest that plants could survive on sunlight and inorganic substances alone. It has since been refined so that plants can be grown with a precise admixture of nutrients. However, hydroponic cultivation is expensive and time-consuming, so it is not viable on a large scale. Some scientists believe that this technique will be especially useful if people ever need to grow plants in space. One spin-off of hydroponic technology has been hydroponic culturing, which identifies the relative importance of various nutrients. In a hydroponic culture, different mineral solutions are applied to the roots of plants: some plants receive a solution in which one mineral is missing, while the other plants receive the full range of minerals. The relative growth of the plants is then observed to indicate the importance of each mineral. For instance, if the leaves of a plant become discolored or are smaller than usual, it would indicate that the omitted mineral is essential to that plant's health.

Genetically modified crops

Genetically modified (GM) crops contain foreign genes, known as transgenes, that give them special properties. Crops have been modified to be hardier, more productive, and even to contain certain pharmaceutical substances. At present, the most popular genetic modifications are for resistance to insects, pathogens, and herbicides. The vast majority of research on genetic modification has been on corn, soybeans, cotton, and other mass-produced plants. The development of recombinant DNA technology has exponentially increased the number of possible modifications. There is a great deal of resistance to GM crops, though it is mainly in developed nations where the need for reliable food sources is less desperate. In impoverished countries, there is great hope that genetic modification can create more nutritious and durable foods.

Genetic modifications for plants

Genetically modified crops promise to improve productivity and nutrition, but many people remain skeptical of their overall impact on the environment. For instance, crops that are modified to tolerate herbicides may eventually spur the development of "super weeds" that are impervious to any herbicide. However, in the short term these crops will reduce the use of herbicides that may be destructive to the environment. Crops that improve resistance to insects may increase agricultural yields and decrease the need for harmful insecticides, but at the same time they may encourage insects to mutate such that they become resistant to common insecticides. For example, many organic farmers rely on the soil bacterium Bt as an insecticide; scientists fear that GM crops will render Bt useless.

There are pros and cons with all GM crops. Those that are grown to be more nutritious will benefit poor people, but may lead to excessive influence for multinational corporations in poor countries. Extremely hardy GM crops may prove to be too durable, to the extent that they drive native species off land that could not be cultivated before.

Bioengineering of livestock

Most people know about genetically modified plants, but few are aware of the similar efforts to develop "enhanced" livestock. One example of bioengineered livestock is the transgenic salmon, in which a growth hormone gene is spliced to a promoter, which encourages transcription of the growth hormone gene. The result is a fish that grows throughout the year and thus reaches a harvestable size much faster. Another example of bioengineered livestock is the Enviropig, which was created in the lab of a Canadian university. The Enviropig has a phytase gene that diminishes the amount of phosphorous in the pig's excrement, thereby reducing the environmental impact of pig farming. Biotechnology has also been used to identify popular and lucrative breeds, like the Angus cow. Bioengineering has often been controversial, as in the case of bovine growth hormones, which increase the growth and milk production of cows but also necessitate the use of more antibiotics on the farm. Many people are concerned that feeding more antibiotics to food animals will decrease the effectiveness of these drugs for people.

Aquaculture

Aquaculture is any cultivation of marine life in an artificial setting. Aquaculture may include fish, shellfish, and even aquatic plants. This practice has become extremely popular in the past few decades, as the market for certain species has increased while natural supplies have shrunk. Critics of aquaculture claim that it causes the rapid expansion of some populations, which puts stress on other parts of the marine ecosystem. Also, aquaculture is commonly practiced in estuaries and lagoons, which have more stagnant water and are therefore more likely to be polluted. There is a growing movement to promote aquaculture in curated environments several miles out at sea. This is called open-ocean aquaculture. Another potential improvement to aquaculture as it is currently practiced would be a greater focus on herbivorous species, which do not wreak such havoc on the ecosystem when they are encouraged to propagate.

Practice Test

Practice Questions

1. Analog NTSC video uses which kind of scanning?
   a. Aliasing
   b. Interlaced
   c. Progressive
   d. Vectorscope

2. A wooden jewelry box is handmade with dovetailed joints. Which kind of wood is most appropriate to use while making the box?
   a. Cedar
   b. Balsa
   c. Birch
   d. Pine

3. A VU meter is used to monitor the audio of a student television talk show. While announcers are speaking, the signal should be adjusted to which portion of the scale?
   a. Near the bottom
   b. To about one-third
   c. Just below the red area
   d. In the red area

4. Which of the following is used to measure the ratio of volts to amps?
   a. Degrees
   b. Joules
   c. Ohms
   d. Watts

5. Students are planning to assemble and operate a small gasoline engine. Which safety concern should have the highest priority?
   a. An open fuel tank could release sickening fumes.
   b. Fingers could be injured if caught in the gears.
   c. Spilled liquids may cause a short in the starter.
   d. The exhaust fumes require adequate ventilation.

6. Students using table-mounted power tools are required to tie back long hair. What is the primary danger if this rule is ignored?
   a. Corrosive fluids spilled on hair could cause permanent damage.
   b. Hair may become caught and pulled by the machinery.
   c. Long hair presents an unprofessional appearance.
   d. Vision may be obscured by hair falling across the eyes.

- 74 -

7. A block of modeling clay should be stored in a way that minimizes the evaporation of moisture. Which shape is best suited for this purpose?
    a. Cylinder
    b. Flattened
    c. Pyramid
    d. Sphere

8. A class activity involves flying model rockets. Which safety mishap is most likely to occur?
    a. Exhaust fumes may cause fires.
    b. Ignition may cause electrocution.
    c. Noise may cause hearing loss.
    d. The rocket body could explode.

9. Which product is likely to include a material safety data sheet?
    a. Computer
    b. Lumber
    c. Paint thinner
    d. Razor blade

10. Which division of colors is most commonly used for video production?
    a. Cyan, magenta, and green
    b. Cyan, magenta, and yellow
    c. Red, green, and blue
    d. Red, yellow, and blue

11. The generation of hydroelectric energy depends primarily on which physical force?
    a. Combustion
    b. Gravity
    c. Heat
    d. Radiation

12. What is meant by the word fossil in the phrase fossil fuel?
    a. It can be put into storage for a long time.
    b. It is an outdated way of generating power.
    c. It is the remains of ancient organisms.
    d. It occurs in sediments containing fossils.

13. Why is "light sweet crude" the most economically valuable form of petroleum?
    a. It is easily mined.
    b. It can be refined efficiently.
    c. It produces less pollution as fuel.
    d. It yields a higher-energy fuel.

14. The length of a shipping container is 3 times the width, while the depth is 1.5 times the width. What is the depth if the length is 226 cm?
    a. 113 cm
    b. 169.5 cm
    c. 452 cm
    d. 508.5 cm

15. How causes the filament of an incandescent bulb to turn electrical current into light?
    a. Combustion
    b. Excitation
    c. Oxidation
    d. Resistance

16. Electricity from an array of wind generators pumps water into a dam. As electricity is demanded by users, it is generated by hydroelectric power. Which statement describes the greatest limitation to this system?
    a. Consumer demand is limited.
    b. Little electricity is generated.
    c. Much pollution is generated.
    d. The amount of water is limited.

17. Which characteristic distinguishes the Engineering Method from the Scientific Method?
    a. Creative input
    b. Evaluation of data
    c. Solving a problem
    d. Testing a hypothesis

18. Which document is most important for retracing steps taken in previous work?
    a. An engineer's logbook
    b. Expense account records
    c. A personnel roster
    d. Orders from customers

19. Which design is best suited for a two-dimensional diagram?
    a. Architectural plans
    b. Circuit board
    c. Combustion engine
    d. Microwave oven

20. Most modern computers operate with which number system?
    a. Base 2
    b. Base 10
    c. Base 12
    d. Base 60

21. A student is deciding between the pursuit of Technology class and school athletics. What should be the primary factor in a teacher's advice?
    a. Addressing diversity needs
    b. Filling the class quorum
    c. Needs of the sports team
    d. The student's aspirations

22. What is the conventional method for turning heat into electricity?
    a. Steam turbine
    b. Thermal diode
    c. Radiation
    d. Transduction

- 76 -

23. Which factor would likely cause a braking system to overheat?
   a. Excess friction
   b. Excess slope
   c. Lack of electricity
   d. Lack of fuel

24. "Proper grounding" is a term used in which field of engineering?
   a. Aviation
   b. Construction
   c. Electric
   d. Plumbing

25. Who would be involved in building a bridge?
   a. Aerospace engineer
   b. Agricultural engineer
   c. Chemical engineer
   d. Civil engineer

26. Which department of an engineering firm would arrange the purchase of building materials?
   a. Design
   b. Marketing
   c. Operations
   d. Sales

27. The results of a stress test yield a bell curve. What is meant by the term standard deviation?
   a. Proportion of non-average data
   b. Range from least to greatest
   c. Most likely result
   d. Least likely result

28. An engineer discovers that substances used by an employer are harmful. Which is the greatest responsibility?
   a. Company profits
   b. Employer's reputation
   c. Harm to people
   d. Progress of science

29. When should high-carbon steel be favored over stainless steel?
   a. When it will come in contact with food
   b. When it's necessary to have something that's easy to weld
   c. When it's necessary to have something with good heat resistance
   d. When it's necessary to have something that maintains sharpness

30. Mass is measured with which unit?
   a. Grams
   b. Joules
   c. Ounces
   d. Newtons

- 77 -

31. A radian is a length equal to which part of a circle?
    a. Circumference
    b. Circumference ÷ pi
    c. Radius
    d. Radius x 2 x pi

32. Which amount has five significant digits?
    a. About 308.00
    b. About 30800
    c. Exactly 308.00
    d. Exactly 30800

33. Which field is most concerned with lightweight materials?
    a. Aerospace
    b. Agriculture
    c. Chemistry
    d. Construction

34. Which technology-oriented profession involves the most hands-on labor?
    a. Operations
    b. Engineering
    c. Management
    d. Sales

35. When data from a conventional square grid is graphed on a logarithmic grid, which option describes what may happen?
    a. Curves become lines.
    b. Exponents become powers of one.
    c. Lines become curves.
    d. Powers of one become exponents.

36. Traffic barriers on public roads are ideally designed to do what?
    a. Absorb impact
    b. Decrease traffic flow
    c. Direct traffic flow
    d. Resist impact

37. Which department of an engineering firm is responsible for gauging customer needs?
    a. Accounting
    b. Management
    c. Marketing
    d. Sales

38. Which Internet resource is a good reference material for a student report?
    a. Discussion group post
    b. Manufacturer's website
    c. User-modifiable encyclopedia
    d. Video gaming sites

- 78 -

X ✱39. A chart of data from a student experiment displays an S-shaped curve. Which degree of equation could model the data on a graphing program?
    a. y = x
    b. y = x2
    c. y = x3
    d. y = x4

40. Where does the physical reaction that propels a rocket or jet primarily take place?
    a. Where the exhaust hits the open air
    b. In the forward area of combustion
    c. In the nozzle where gases escape
    d. In the oxygen delivery system

41. Thin sheets of wood are layered with the grain alternating to form veneer-core plywood. What is the reason for alternating the grain?
    a. Creative design
    b. Low cost
    c. Prevent warping
    d. Rot resistance

42. The functioning of hydraulic systems depends on which principle?
    a. Liquids cannot be compressed.
    b. Liquids cannot be ionized.
    c. Liquids cannot be pressurized.
    d. Liquids cannot be vaporized.

43. Which statement describes the typical operation of an assembly line?
    a. Product moves between factories.
    b. Product moves between workers.
    c. Workers move between factories.
    d. Workers move between products.

44. The kerf produced by a saw is mainly determined by which factor?
    a. The angle of the cut
    b. The thickness of the saw
    c. The type of saw used
    d. The type of wood used

✱✱45. Which scale is most appropriate for printed architectural plans showing a house?
    a. 1:3
    b. 1:10
    c. 1:50   Nifty fifty
    d. 1:200

46. Which material is appropriate for casting?
    a. Cloth
    b. Resin
    c. Stone
    d. Wood

47. Why does a bar code scanner use a hologram?
    a. For identity protection
    b. To scan holographic codes
    c. To scan in many directions
    d. For user safety

48. Which consumer appliance likely requires the highest outlet voltage?
    a. An air conditioner
    b. A computer
    c. A photocopier
    d. A vacuum cleaner

49. Which of the following options is a typical function for a capacitor?
    a. Alters voltage level
    b. Resists current
    c. Stores electrical charge
    d. Turns current into light

50. Which temperature is most commonly used for soldering?
    a. 180 degrees Celsius
    b. 320 degrees Celsius
    c. 400 degrees Celsius
    d. 550 degrees Celsius

51. Excess current in electronic components may cause what harmful factor?
    a. Cold
    b. Dryness
    c. Heat
    d. Moisture

52. Which condition is most important to help concrete harden properly?
    a. Cold
    b. Dryness
    c. Heat
    d. Moisture

53. Which saw is appropriate for cutting metal?
    a. Chain saw
    b. Cold saw
    c. Hand saw
    d. Rip saw

54. Which of the following options is a characteristic of flash drives?
    a. Uses electricity to retain memory
    b. Single writing session
    c. Spinning disc
    d. Solid state components

55. Pieces of wooden frame for the walls of a house are commonly cut to which degree of accuracy?
    a. 0.005 inch
    b. 0.01 inch
    c. 1/32 inch
    d. 1/4 inch

56. Which choice is a positive characteristic typical of concrete?
    a. Good compressive strength
    b. Good tensile strength
    c. Resistance to cold
    d. Resistance to heat

57. The word carbon in carbon steel refers to what?
    a. Alloys
    b. Finish
    c. Magnetism
    d. Reproduction

58. A miter joint is most often used for what kind of woodworking?
    a. Finished furniture
    b. The frame of a wall
    c. Shipping crates
    d. Warehouse pallets

59. What is the primary reason that engineers sign, stamp, or otherwise certify their work?
    a. To encourage follow-up business
    b. To protect intellectual property
    c. To receive payments and royalties
    d. To verify the origin and quality of work

60. Students present when arc-welding is conducted are required to look away, even if they are standing several meters distant. What is this safety practice intended to prevent?
    a. Burns caused by sparks
    b. Eye damage due to brightness
    c. Inhalation of contaminants
    d. Making the operator nervous

61. Which material is most effective for safety gloves used with power tools?
    a. Cotton
    b. Leather
    c. Rubber
    d. Vinyl

62. What most commonly provides the main structural support for the foundation of a ground-floor wall?
    a. Concrete
    b. Soil
    c. Steel
    d. Stone

63. Which option is the primary ingredient in drywall?
   a. Ash
   b. Cement
   c. Gypsum
   d. Paper

64. The walls of a basement are usually positioned to extend below what?
   a. Airline
   b. Frostline
   c. Waterline
   d. Windline

65. What is a practical purpose for the glass walls of skyscrapers?
   a. Decoration
   b. Insulation
   c. Privacy
   d. Support

66. Which option is the most common function of a multitester?
   a. Heat
   b. Light
   c. Moisture
   d. Resistance

67. What is an example of a substrate?
   a. A Printed circuit board
   b. An underground pipe
   c. An underwater pump
   d. A varnish or paint

68. What is a good reason to use a patent instead of a trade secret for intellectual property?
   a. For licensing to other companies
   b. For long-term exclusive use
   c. If the invention is a process
   d. If the technique is not novel

69. Which tool is a surveyor's compass that distinguishes between magnetic north and true north?
   a. Theodolite
   b. Transit
   c. Vernier
   d. Wye level

70. An industrial standard most likely comes from what source?
   a. A single company or firm
   b. A consumer protection group
   c. International legislation
   d. A professional organization

- 82 -

71. An older machine in the school workshop may be replaced for $1,000, or the school can continue to repair it for about $50 a year. The older machine will probably become obsolete in five years, while any replacement will become obsolete in ten years. Which option is the most economical solution?
    a. Buy a replacement immediately
    b. Keep the older machine for five years
    c. Keep the older machine for ten years
    d. Keep the older machine indefinitely

72. Which option best fits the most prevalent definition of biotechnology?
    a. An alteration of chromosomes
    b. Airplane bodies that mimic birds
    c. A new way of sealing wood
    d. Developing artificial limbs

73. Which classification includes plotter printers?
    a. Font
    b. Raster
    c. Typeface
    d. Vector

74. A jigsaw will be used to make a cut in the middle of a board, without touching the edges of the board. Which step should be taken before using the saw?
    a. Apply any varnish or paint to be used.
    b. Attach any accessories for the piece.
    c. Drill holes between the endpoints of the cut.
    d. Sand the surface of the wood.

75. Which activity requires a dust mask?
    a. Applying paint
    b. Cutting sheet metal
    c. Sanding wood
    d. Tanning leather

76. Which of the following options is a role of project management?
    a. Deciding who's right for a job
    b. Determining the pace of work
    c. Finding the best materials to use
    d. Interpreting customer wishes

77. In the modern practice of manufacturing, individual copies of a given component are virtually identical. How does this aid the assembly of components into a finished product?
    a. Individual parts are interchangeable
    b. Scale drawings can be made
    c. The finished products are identical
    d. Quality control is assured

- 83 -

78. When a teacher wishes to contact a student's parents, what is an advantage to using notifications on paper rather than electronic communications?
   a. A parent might not have access to electronic communications.
   b. Electronic data can be falsified more easily than paper.
   c. Handwritten notes are more personable and friendly.
   d. Paper documents are seen as more important and binding.

79. The storage of digital video on a computer takes up more memory than does storage of digital audio. Which ratio best approximates the difference of scale?
   a. 10:1
   b. 200:1
   c. 1,000:1
   d. 5,000:1

80. Which activity is most likely to be restricted by local safety ordinances?
   a. Applying chemical surface treatments
   b. Flying combustion-driven model rockets
   c. Radio or television transmissions
   d. Using outdoor power tools

81. Which of the following best describes why an engineering degree includes requirements for humanities courses?
   a. Better communication with clients
   b. Empathy for environmental regulations
   c. Improved grammar and spelling
   d. Understanding the history of an industry

82. Which subject of study best adheres to the general curriculum of technology education?
   a. Physics of astronomy
   b. Production of video games
   c. Soil erosion and retention
   d. Standardized assessments

83. Which of the following options is an example of industrial biotechnology?
   a. Blood plasma substitutes
   b. Enzymes used as catalysts
   c. Improved seed crops
   d. New cancer treatments

84. Which self-contained system is the most energy-efficient?
   a. A diesel engine
   b. A gasoline engine
   c. An electric engine powered by a diesel generator
   d. An electric engine powered by a gasoline generator

85. Which aspect of quality control determines the validity of quality standards?
   a. Company quality
   b. Failure testing
   c. Statistical control
   d. Total quality control

- 84 -

86. Which is a likely example of a marketing department's directives or information provided to an engineering department?
    a. Availability of materials
    b. Investment resources
    c. Cost of the product
    d. Relevant safety standards

87. The sizes of paper for printing are addressed by which standards organization?
    a. American National Standards Institute
    b. Institute of Electrical and Electronic Engineers
    c. National Institute of Standards and Technology
    d. Institute of Nuclear Materials Management

88. Your technology class requires students to provide combination locks for securely storing project materials. Which type of lock is most advisable?
    a. Electronic keypad
    b. Multiple dial
    c. Push-button
    d. Single dial

89. Lumber is often sold in a nominal size that is not exactly the same as the actual size. Which statement describes the actual dimensions in comparison to the nominal dimensions?
    a. Length may be longer, and width and thickness may be longer
    b. Length may be longer, while width and thickness may be shorter
    c. Length may be shorter, and width and thickness may be shorter
    d. Length may be shorter, while width and thickness may be longer

90. Which option is a common use for an oscilloscope?
    a. Determining mechanical rotations
    b. Displaying the wave patterns of a signal
    c. Finding small surface defects
    d. Viewing the interior of a machine

91. Powder painting is an industrial method that uses an electrostatic charge. What is the primary reason for using such a charge?
    a. Corrosion resistance
    b. Demagnetization
    c. Easy paint removal
    d. Improved adhesion

92. Some manufacturing processes are conducted in an atmosphere of nitrogen and argon. What is the primary reason for using this mixture instead of ordinary air?
    a. Avoiding oxidation
    b. Better calcification
    c. Moisturization
    d. Pressure regulation

- 85 -

93. In which of the following are fiber optics commonly used?
    a. Agriculture
    b. Communication
    c. Magnification
    d. Textiles

94. Plans for a vehicle are drawn to 1:192 scale. If one part of the vehicle measures 3/16 inch on the plans, what is the measurement of the actual part?
    a. 3 inches
    b. 6 inches
    c. 3 feet
    d. 6 feet

95. Chemical vapor deposition is a manufacturing process that produces thin films. Which industry most commonly uses this technique?
    a. Automotive
    b. Furniture
    c. Motion pictures
    d. Semiconductors

96. One gear in a machine has 25 teeth, and turns another gear with 36 teeth. Which option properly expresses the gear ratio?
    a. 0.69:1
    b. 0.83:1
    c. 1.2:1
    d. 1.44:1

97. Video may be recorded with a subject in front of a green-colored screen, which allows an additional video source to be added to the picture. Which statement describes the most relevant operating principle?
    a. The added video appears in a corner.
    b. The camera ignores the green screen.
    c. The focal length of the lens changes.
    d. The subject appears in a green light.

98. Many varieties of sandpaper are made to be used while moistened with water. What is the primary reason for this practice?
    a. Abrasion
    b. Cleaning
    c. Lubrication
    d. Sealing

99. Epoxy adhesives are supplied in two separate containers that are mixed together before application. What is the primary reason for this step?
    a. The compound contracts after mixing.
    b. The compound expands after mixing.
    c. The compound hardens after mixing.
    d. The compound softens after mixing.

- 86 -

1/1

100. Biotechnology has produced results such as improved varieties of vegetable crops. This is mainly accomplished by which method?
   a. Irradiation of harvested crops
   b. Monitoring pests by video
   c. Transferring genetic material
   d. Using specially enriched soils

89/100 = 2nd Round

63/100 = 1st Round

Net Gain = 26 Points

Answers and Explanations

1. B: Analog NTSC (National Television Standards Commission) video scans in alternating, interlaced lines designed to handle moving images without a flickering effect. Computer CRT monitors often use progressive scanning of consecutive lines, while many modern flat-panel digital displays can display both formats. Failure to maintain the relationship of continuously flowing data can lead to aliasing, where a given frame's information becomes confused with that of another frame. Improper conversion between formats can produce aliasing. One must be aware of the formats used by each piece of equipment and adjust formats as necessary.

2. C: Birch is a hardwood suitable for intricate, durable joint-work. While many kinds of lumber may be machine-made into dovetailed joints, working by hand requires a durable wood that is less likely to chip. Balsa is technically a hardwood by botanical definition, but has the soft characteristics associated with softwoods. Cedar and birch are softwoods with softer, more easily breakable characteristics. Therefore while cedar, birch, and pine could under the proper circumstances be used for intricate joint-work, only birch is well-suited for this application in handmade student work. Machine-worked pieces are more common in an industrial context.

3. B: Speaking voices adjusted about one-third of the way up the scale produce occasional peaks just below the undesirable red area. Therefore this is the highest level that can be maintained. If the needle or digital indicator is near the bottom, the sound level will be too low, and if it is amplified by another component afterwards the amount of usable data will also be correspondingly too low. The sound levels generated by many forms of music do not have as much variation as the human voice, and so the highest possible level is just below the undesirable red area.

4. C: Voltage divided by amperage is equal to ohms of resistance. Division is a kind of ratio, which can be stated or written in several ways. The measurement of watts contributes to the measurement of amps (or amperage), but in and of itself cannot be stated as part of this particular ratio. Joules are a measurement of energy, which may include electricity as well as all other forms of energy, but do not constitute a term of this ratio by itself. The degree is a term with a variety of uses and definitions, but is not a term of this ratio.

5. D: Exhaust fumes are an ever-present concern, while the others are incidents that might or might not occur. A combustion engine of any kind produces fumes which can rapidly cause health damage, brain damage or death if allowed to fill an inadequately ventilated space. Therefore activities of this kind are usually conducted near an open garage door or loading dock if not out-of-doors. A situation guaranteed to happen--the production of fumes--is of higher priority than incidental dangers.

6. B: Long hair may fall into the machinery when an operator leans forward. This may cause the hair to be caught in gears or similar moving parts, causing the hair to be pulled and subsequently causing injury, either by pulling the hair from the scalp or by pulling the operator towards and into the machinery. The other listed options include obscuring of

vision, something that could be a problem but which depends upon the individual. Health damage or property damage due to spills of corrosives are not limited to hair.

7. D: Of all three-dimensional shapes, a sphere has the lowest surface area, minimizing the escape of moisture. Moisture evaporates from the surface of an object, so the greater the surface area the greater the potential for loss or moisture. While storage in this ideal shape is not always possible, the question asks which option is theoretically most desirable. An analogy can be made to rounded blocks of cheese, having flattened tops and bottoms to allow easy stacking, while spheroid elements are incorporated where possible along the edges. If the block of clay is flattened, surface area is maximized and so drying would be accelerated.

8. A: Model rockets produce flammable exhaust, while the other incidents are very unlikely. Ignition is usually accomplished by flashlight-type batteries having too little power to be dangerous. The level of noise produced could be a concern if involving constant, long-term exposure, but this is not likely with school projects. The level of pressure created by a model rocket is not enough to cause explosions, an attribute of liquid fuel devices rather than a model rocket's solid fuel. Nevertheless, the danger of fires caused by flammable exhaust are significant, so care must be taken.

9. C: Chemicals are usually provided with a material safety data sheet. Liquid paint thinner fits this definition and so is required by law to have appropriate warnings, although the information provided with consumer products is not likely to be as copious as with substances sold for commercial industrial use. The other options do of course contain chemicals of one kind or another, but the information given in the question does not make this necessity as likely as for the paint thinner.

10. C: Video commonly uses a red/green/blue color wheel, while the others are used for printing and for traditional artwork. The reason for this is that the human eye has particular attenuations that are not exactly the same as the theoretical attributes of light wavelengths themselves. Video is designed to produce as realistic a picture as possible, and so must be engineered to follow human characteristics as closely as possible. Human eyes can perceive differences in shades of green more accurately than shades of yellow.

11. B: The downward flow of water from a dam spins turbines to produce electricity. This requires the water to be above the turbines, so that gravity pulls the water downward. Many other forms of electricity generation using water function by means of steam pressure, where the heat from combustion, radiation, or geothermal sources turns water into steam. In such case the steam rises upward rather than downward, against and in spite of the force of gravity. In both scenarios, pressure against the turbine is exploited to make the turbine spin.

12. C: Deposits of petroleum and coal are the mineralized remains of life dating from the distant past. Intact fossils of bone or plant impressions are in fact often found in coal deposits, but this alone does not identify a given sediment as coal or other fossil fuel. Nor is it the definition of a coal deposit: a fossil fuel deposit might not contain any recognizable organisms. Fossil fuels can be stored without spoilage for long periods; however, this does not pertain to the term. Likewise, the advancement of renewable resources could someday render fossils fuels, but this is not the meaning of the term.

13. B: The term "light sweet crude" means raw petroleum with relatively few impurities such as sulfur. This makes it easier and less costly to refine. While fewer impurities means that more energy-yielding fuel may be derived from it, the end products are similar in energy potential. Likewise in terms of pollution: a greater mass of by-products is produced when petroleum with more impurities is refined, but this does not necessarily reflect the pollution potential of the end product. Neither does the difficulty of extracting the petroleum from the ground necessarily correlate to this classification.

14. A: The information in the question is stated in terms of width, but width itself is not given. Therefore the provided actual measurement, length, must be divided by 3, and then multiplied by 1.5. Alternately, 3 could be compared to 1.5 to find the ratio of length to depth, 2:1. The incorrect options are derived from applying the information incorrectly, or by transposing the data for width with the data for length. Other mistakes could include multiplying when the information calls for division, or reversing the numerator with the denominator of a ratio.

15. D: Current passes though the filament of a conventional electric bulb, meeting resistance from the composition of said filament. This resistance produces both heat and light on the non-visible portions of the spectrum, both of which are usually undesirable by-products, and visible light, the intended product. Oxidation and combustion are prevented from interfering with the process by enclosing the filament into the near-vacuum of a glass bulb. Electrical fluorescent light bulbs generate light by the excitation of gases with an electric current passing through it, producing fewer by-products and consuming less power.

16. D: The question describes a way of saving wind power, generated when the wind is blowing, for use when the wind is insufficient for consumer needs. The large-scale demand by consumers is the motivation for building this system, rather than a limitation. The system is intended to produce power without the copious pollution of other systems, such as burning fossil fuels. The limits of the system are ultimately the amount of water available as well as the capacity of the dam and of natural waterways downstream to accept the outflow without flooding.

17. C: The Engineering Method is an overview of design and testing processes, which usually includes application of the Scientific Method. Therefore any element of the Scientific Method, such as creative input, evaluation of data, or testing a hypothesis, may be considered part of the Engineering Method as well, rather than something which distinguishes the two concepts. The difference is that the Engineering Method revolves around solving problems, such as filling a need for a new kind of machine, or overcoming a specific difficulty or failure. The Scientific Method does not explicitly address such needs.

18. A: All of the listed options could conceivably be used to retrace the steps taken by an engineering process. Expense accounts could show how resources are allocated, personnel records may show who was involved in a specific project, and orders from customers could be compared to steps taken in filling those orders. However, these are all incidental uses which may or may not be useful. An engineer's logbook is specifically intended to allow retracing the steps taken in a project.

19. B: A circuit board is built on a flat substrate. While it often may contain some overlap of components, the majority of components are aligned on a single two-dimensional plane. All of the listed options can be and commonly are depicted in two dimensions, but require a

greater extent of cross-sections to depict all relevant details. An architectural plan for a building could include a series of flat blueprints, side views, and three-dimensional models. The engine and oven might be suitably depicted by a series of exploded views as well as flat plane views.

20. A: The vast majority of modern electronic computers are binary. All values are expressed as "on" or "off." As numerals, this is shown as 0 or 1. Subsequently, all values are combinations of powers of two. All other numerical values, such as the base-10 system in common usage, must be derived or translated from base-2 numbers. Base-12 or base-60 (sexagesimal) numbers are a traditional form still used for the degrees of a circle, longitude and latitude, and clocks. A binary must translate binary values into these systems if needed.

21. D: The needs, aspirations, and qualifications of students are the fundamental reason for the existence of the education system. Attaining a diverse student body is a legitimate goal, but should not determine an individual student's path. Class quorums are a practical reality, but ideally are not the determining factor. Although difficult decisions must be made when too many students want a particular class, this should not be the deciding factor when determining the ideal path for a given student. The needs of the sports team are not directly relevant to how well-suited a student is for an unrelated technology class.

22. A: Thermal heat sources, whether artificially made or taken from natural sources, are usually turned into electrical power by heating water into steam, which rises under pressure to spin a turbine, producing electricity from physical rotation. Thermal diodes are experimental devices that generate electricity with solid-state electronics, but this is to date purely experimental. Transduction refers to one kind of signal being converted into another type of signal, rather than the generation of usable energy, although the signal itself may require energy such as electricity.

23. A: Most braking systems operate on a principle of applying friction to a spinning disc. Friction causes heat, which may prove to be excessive, particularly if the components are poorly maintained, or if the system is used in situations which exceed the design specifications. A vehicle moving down a steep slope may find itself in such a situation of being compelled to apply the brakes in an overly forceful manner, but this is an indirect cause. Many braking systems employ power to operate, so a power failure could cause the system to operate improperly, but this does not the primary cause of overheating per se.

24. C: Many electrical systems rely on grounding, the directing of excess current into the earth (or in the case of airplanes an inert portion of the vehicle), in order to prevent overload. The term may also refer to a base value of voltage, but again this is a term applying to electrical systems. Plumbing and construction projects or systems frequently employ electrical systems which in turn require grounding, but these applications are secondary to the electrical systems themselves. A malfunctioning airplane may be "grounded," or prevented from flying, but this is not referred to as "proper grounding."

25. D: Civil engineering refers to large-scale projects that are used by many segments of society, such as roads or sewer systems. Many of these are government-directed and government-financed, then contracted to private industry. A civil engineer may be employed by either party. The other options are professions which do not involve road or bridge construction at all, except in the secondary sense that an agricultural engineer may

plan a farm which includes a bridge, or a chemical engineer may contribute to the development of construction materials.

26. C: A design department might purchase materials for experiments or demonstrations, but not for the actual use of the product for customers, in which case it would be more than a design department. Marketing and sales are both areas concerned with selling products or finding potential customers, but not in acquiring materials. An operations department is concerned with using or implementing products, so the acquisition of materials is central to its mission.

27. A: Deviation means variance from a central tendency such as mean, median, or mode. That is, results that do not match the results defined in this way. Standard deviation is a measure of how many results fit the central tendency versus how many do not and by what margin. In particular, the measure is useful when most results are clustered around the center and drop-off in either direction. The range of results, as well as the most or least likely results, relate mathematically to standard deviation but are not by definition the same as the term itself.

28. C: If a substance, other product, or service is potentially harmful to people, care must be taken to either remove it from use or issue an appropriate warning that allows users to make an educated decision. Beyond purely ethical considerations, employees who knowingly manufacture goods with a potential for harm subsequently open the company up to disrepute among customers, costly litigation, or legislated legal censure. The theoretical advancement of scientific knowledge is not a legitimate or acknowledged defense against such failures.

29. D: Iron that is alloyed with carbon in the manufacturing process is stronger and retains its shape better than other varieties such stainless steel. A sharp blade is an example of this shape retention. The other options are examples of situations requiring the attributes of stainless steel: heat resistance is generally superior to high-carbon alloys, as is ease of welding. While neither variety is harmful to food, the ease of cleaning stainless steel is an advantage in the context of food preparation. Carbon steel must be protected from moisture, which is often accomplished with oils that should not contact food.

30. A: The gram, as well as related metric terms such as kilogram or microgram, is defined by the SI (International System) as measuring only mass, not weight. Newtons are the unit for considering both mass and gravity in the form of weight. In the U.S. customary system, ounces measure weight rather than mass. Joules are a measure of energy, not weight or mass, although relativity physics compares mass to energy. Nevertheless, it is common to find grams described as measuring weight in casual usage, so making the distinction for students is important.

31. C: A radian is a portion of a circle's circumference equal in length to the radius, although the radius is a line segment while the radian is a curved arc. The radian is the SI (International System) preference for measuring circumference, although the sexagesimal 360-degree circle is still in common use. Radius ? 2 ? pi is equal to the full circumference. Circumference ÷ pi equals two radians, so this option would read circumference ÷ pi ÷ 2 if correct. Circumference by itself is equal to one radian ? 2 ? pi.

32. D: Significant digits are sometimes described as non-zero values, although this may or may not be the case. The difference is whether zero is an exact amount or the truncated portion of an estimate. If we read "five million cars" in an article, it can be usually be assumed that the amount is not really an even 5,000,000, but simply shorthand for an approximate amount. Trailing zeroes after a decimal are usually omitted entirely, but are sometimes used to note statistical accuracy. Although this means that results of 308.01 are improbable, it is not the same as an actual value.

33. A: Many if not all schools of engineering are concerned with finding lightweight materials in some context. In the construction of a building for instance, if the first story of a building can support a given weight, the second story can be bigger it the materials used to construct it are lighter. In agriculture, the particular composition of cropland may support vehicles of a certain weight, but heavier machines become bogged down. However, the priority for lightweight materials in aerospace is of primary importance, because the available energy to a flying craft is very limited.

34. A: Operations departments are typically charged with implementing, using, and maintaining the designs and solutions of engineers. This may involve for instance the actual operation of a power station, updating components of a computer server, or similar hands-on tasks. Management often is involved only peripherally with these activities, while sales departments usually have little to do with such operations. The distinction is important to technology education because students should pursue careers where they will feel comfortable. Familiarity with the actual daily activities of persons in a profession will help students make an informed choice.

35. A: Logarithmic or semi-logarithmic grids have, instead of the identical squares found in a conventional Cartesian grid, rows of progressively compressed rectangles with units to match. The purpose of this arrangement is to allow non-linear expressions to be graphed as a straight line, which results in more information to be placed upon a single sheet of paper (or computer screen). Otherwise, expressions containing exponents of two or greater would be curves, which would require an inordinately large graph to depict fully in a way that could be easily used.

36. A: Traffic barriers, such as plastic barrels, posts, or metal bars, are designed to crumple upon impact, much as the front and rear sections of a car have "crumple zones" designed to do the same thing. Such a violent collapse absorbs considerable energy, which is that much less destructive energy passed on to the occupants of the vehicles. The question specifies public roads because privately constructed barriers are often made without such considerations, sometimes being intended to stop thieves from crashing through the glass walls of a retail store, rather than accidental impacts.

37. C: All of the listed options are concerned with customer satisfaction to some extent; however, marketing is the department that explicitly exists for this purpose. Management decides the priorities of marketing, accounting determines the economic implications of a project, and sales finds the customer. Marketing is a topic appropriate for technology classes, because engineering exists to fill needs or wants. Marketing personnel thus often work with engineers to find a feasible solution to the demands of customers and are included as engineering-related career paths.

38. B: Discussion group posts are good for finding exhaustive information not available elsewhere, but are altered frequently. Therefore they might not be there when you need the information later. User-created encyclopedias have similar advantages and drawbacks, and both can be unreliable sources. Video gaming sites could be a resource for student investigation of computer-graphic techniques, but would be a distraction in most other contexts. A relevant manufacturer's site can be an ideal source for technical information. Competency 009

39. C: Expressions without exponents (having only powers of one) are said to be linear because they produce straight lines when graphed on a Cartesian grid. A second degree expression (or equation or inequality or function) produces a curved parabola, while a third degree expression (so named for the highest exponent in any term) produces an S-shaped graph. Some graphing programs can produce both a graph and an equation for a given set of data, although real-life data is often too messy to show the underlying principles clearly for educational purposes.

40. B: All of the options contribute in some way to the propulsion of the vehicle. Until about a century ago, it was thought that the exhaust hitting the open air was the site of this physical reaction. The nozzle leading from the combustion chamber to the exhaust creates a low pressure area which allows the vehicle to be propelled in the opposite direction, but it is the forward portion of the combustion chamber where the high pressure builds, moving the vehicle forward. The oxygen delivery system contributes to this, but is only a portion of the said high-pressure region.

41. C: Wood tends to warp in certain directions, which are determined by the grain. When pieces of wood are set together with the grain alternating in perpendicular directions, the warping of one piece is compensated by adjacent pieces warping in other directions. In the case of plywood, this is not outwardly visible and so does not function as a design element. While low cost is often an incentive to use plywood, it does not contribute to this practice, nor is vulnerability to rot affected.

42. A: Because liquids cannot be compressed, they convey pressure very effectively. That is, the volume of a liquid body cannot change by mechanical pressure alone. When liquid on one end of a tube is pushed inward, an equal amount of liquid is pushed out of the other side (if we assume that the tube has perfect integrity). Thus, it is subject to pressure but not to compression. Ionization (affecting electrical balances) and vaporization (liquid becoming gas) are possible but not directly relevant to the operation of hydraulics.

43. B: All of the options are potential and real descriptions of the operation of assembly lines. The adoption of outsourcing has increased the amount of product moving from factory to factory before completion; some functions are so specialized that a given single worker may be required at different location. However, the fundamental principle of this manufacturing method is that products are more efficiently moved than are workers or their work stations and tools.

44. B: Kerf refers to the gap left by a saw as it moves through the material being cut. A thin saw produces a thin kerf, while a thick saw with compound rows of teeth results in a wide kerf. The exact relationship of kerf to saw thickness is also affected by vibrations or unwanted motion, but these are minor differences. The other options are minor factors when compared to saw thickness as well.

- 94 -

45. C: Architectural plans are most commonly printed on paper measuring about one square yard. A residential house, measuring perhaps 20-60 feet across, would need to be scaled down by a ratio of 1:20 to 1:100 in order to fit on the paper. This range therefore includes the scales most commonly used by the construction industry. A plan drawn to a scale of 1:50 fits within the range, while a scale of 1:200 would be more appropriate for larger buildings or complexes. Scales of 1:3 or 1:10 might show a small part of the building.

46. B: Casting is the process of liquefying a material, usually accomplished by heat, and then pouring the liquid into a mold. As the liquid cools, it turns into a solid which retains the shape of the mold. Essential to the process is a material which can be liquefied. Resin is a term referring to substances traditionally derived from tree sap, but also including synthetic plastics that behave in a similar manner. Cloth and wood would burn rather than melt if heated in an oxygen atmosphere, while most kinds of stone would crack before melting.

47. B: Early bar code scanners used simple mirrors to bounce a laser beam into the proper angle for crossing a bar code. However, in this set-up the bar code must be held at the exactly correct angle, which is difficult for human operators to accomplish. The use of a holographic surface instead of a mirror splits the single beam into many beams, thus providing many different acceptable angles for passing the bar code. The code itself is not usually a hologram, nor are protection against counterfeit codes or user injury significantly affected.

48. A: There are many appliances sold in the United States with 240-volt rather than 120-volt outlet power requirements. The key differentiating statement in this item is the word consumer, which indicates a domain of products other than industrial or business machinery. Appliances intended to be frequently plugged in and unplugged by the non-expert consumer are usually sold in a 120-volt configuration, including most desk computers, small to mid-sized home or office photocopiers, and vacuum cleaners. Air conditioners, including small window units, are usually sold in a 240-volt configuration.

49. C: A capacitor stores an electric charge, often a very low charge, for electronic components and circuits. The purpose of such a function is to maintain a constant, regulated charge of current when other components on the circuit would otherwise cause undesired variance. The other options include changing instead of maintaining voltage, a function of transformers; the resistance function of resistors; and the production of light, which may be accomplished by a variety of mechanisms such as a light-emitting diode or an incandescent bulb.

50. A: Solder is melted to a temperature of 90 to 450 degrees Celsius, or 200 to 840 degrees Fahrenheit. However, a temperature of 180 to 190 degrees Celsius is the range most typically used. The reason is that the process is usually used to join electrical components or conducting wire. These components would melt or be otherwise damaged if the temperature is too high or alters too rapidly. Higher-end and professional-use soldering guns have a temperature-control mechanism to prevent this, while heat sinks (simple metal clips) are placed around the area to be soldered as a way of absorbing excess heat.

51. C: Excess heat from any source, be it from electrical current or ambient temperature, will damage electronic components; the smoke produced by a fire can do more damage still. Excess cold and dryness could, in certain circumstances, be harmful as well, but these are

not common effects, nor are they the result of excess current. Moisture is a common hazard but is not an effect of excess current. Current that is excessive in terms of voltage, wattage, or the ratio of the two produces heat, which is one of the most common causes of component failure.

52. D: The correct answer may seem counter-intuitive but is a process common to proper use of concrete. The concrete (composed of cement powder mixed with water) must dry out, but doing so too rapidly results in cracks. Therefore an essential step is to continually spray the drying cement with water when ambient moisture is insufficient, or even to suspend a reservoir of water above the cement to be drained upon it as needed. A warm temperature speeds the process and increases strength and is thus desirable. However, this option is not as essential as the presence of adequate moisture.

53. B: A cold saw is a circular saw blade designed to transfer the friction-based heat of cutting to the small bits of metal being sawed away, rather than to the piece of metal being sawed, or to the saw itself. This characteristic is beneficial because otherwise both components become too hot to touch and would otherwise experience the distortion in size and shape that occur when metal is heated. Chainsaws and rip saws are usually designed for cutting wood, while a hand saw could be designed for a variety of uses (although wood is the most common application in this case).

54. D: Although the term solid state was originally intended to distinguish tube-based electronics from modern forms such as transistors, it is commonly used to mean any electronic device with no moving parts. This is an advantage held by USB and other solid-state flash memory devices in contrast to disc or tape drives, which move the storage medium over a reader. Unlike random access memory, a constant current is not required, and unlike read-only memory the medium may be written over many times.

55. D: The degree of accuracy required for the large-scale frames of houses is not very great when compared to most other forms of woodworking. The material is fairly pliable, the lengths involved are large enough to exploit that pliability, and the joints themselves are uncomplicated: the end of one piece is laid against the side of another, while metal struts provide reinforcement. Therefore the accuracy needed, about 1/4 inch, is less exacting than most other kinds of construction or craftwork. The options other than 1/4 inch are appropriate for finer woodwork or for mechanical parts.

56. A: The primary building advantage of concrete is its resistance to high pressures, allowing large loads of weight to be rested upon it or anchored by it. Tensile strength is poor, often requiring use of rebar (joined metal struts centered inside the mass of concrete). Even when rebar is used, the concrete is still very brittle, subject to cracking or breaking off when loads are not properly balanced or become excessive. Extreme temperatures may affect concrete, but are in any case not a factor that distinguishes use of the material.

57. A: The term carbon steel is a reference both to the presence of carbon as an alloy as well as to the relative absence of other alloying substances such as copper. The presence of carbon helps prevent the dislocation of atoms within the steel. The surface finish of products made with these alloys is irrelevant to the term itself, as are the magnetic properties. Use of the term carbon in the context of reproduction was commonly used to refer to carbon paper, an obsolete process predating modern photocopiers.

58. A: A miter joint involves two diagonally cut pieces of wood joined at an angle of about 45 degrees, linking the pieces themselves at an angle typically of 90 degrees. The purpose of such a join is primarily aesthetic rather than functional. This is characteristic of finished pieces, particularly the visible outer surface of these pieces. Shipping crates and warehouse pallets are roughly constructed, while the frame of a wall is usually concealed under plaster, drywall, and paint. Finished pieces of furniture or a picture frame are the most common applications.

59. D: While all of the options are possible results of engineers certifying their work, the specific purpose of this practice is to verify that the engineer is properly certified and otherwise qualified to perform the work, and that the work has been executed in proper fashion. This is commonly accomplished by use of ink stamps, or by a simple signature or initials. The other options are essentially potential beneficial results which could happen as a result of following these conventions, but are not usually the primary means of ensuring such goals.

60. B: All of the options are hazards common to arc welding and other forms of welding. However, it is the brightness of the light created that is dangerous over a distance. Persons who are present in a room or area where arc welding is conducted should wear eye protection. If this is not practical, such as when many persons are present or when the welding is conducted for a brief time, all persons without appropriate eye protection should be required to look away from the light produced by the welding process.

61. B: Leather, or similar materials such as synthetic leather substitutes, is recommended for use with power tools as protective although not invulnerable safety gear. Cotton gloves are used with hand tools and similar labor to prevent simple abrasions rather than forcible cuts or pinches, while rubber, vinyl or similar non-permeable, non-woven materials are used for handling chemicals. However, none of the other options provide the strength to stand up to the possible stresses resulting from common power tools.

62. A: In modern buildings, the frame supports are most commonly held in place by concrete. The concrete may contain steel rebar and stone aggregate, but these are not the primary or definitive components. The employment of a packed-soil foundation alone is an archaic construction method, although soil and rubble infills are often used to buttress the concrete. Steel girders are used extensively as frame supports, but are held by the foundation rather than being the main component of the foundation itself. Stone blocks continue to be used as foundation material in modern times, but are less common than poured concrete.

63. C: The primary component of drywall sheets is a plaster made of gypsum; hence, the common terms gypsum board or plaster board. The gypsum is refined from calcium sulfate and mixed with additives, which may include paper fiber and potash or similar ash-like substances, but these are not the primary component, nor are the sheets of paper which line the side. Cement, when used as a generic term, may describe adhesives used but these are not the main ingredient of the product.

64. B: A building made entirely above the frostline, or lowest depth at which groundwater typically freezes in cold weather, may suffer foundation damage as a result of pressure from expansion and contraction in the surrounding soil as water freezes and unfreezes. Extending the building below this area prevents such damage and is an important reason

- 97 -

why basements are more commonly built in cold climates than in warm ones. The copious presence of groundwater would be a disincentive to building a basement.

65. B: Large buildings with visible exteriors made almost entirely of glass are often considered to be designed as such for aesthetic architectural purposes, although there are practical advantages. One of these is the insulating property of glass, a particularly useful aspect on very tall buildings, where the ambient outside temperatures and wind patterns are irregular and undesirable. Little support is provided by glass walls, so these buildings usually have a core of steel girders. Decoration is by definition not a practical purpose, nor does glass help issues of tenant privacy.

66. D: A multitester (or multimeter) is a handheld electronic instrument used to test several measurements of electrical current, and sometimes other physical phenomena. A great variety of electronic multitesters have been designed and sold for many different specialties of the field. However, most instruments bearing the name are intended to measure voltage, wattage, and resistance. Temperature, humidity, and light are all parameters measured by certain specialized models, but are by no means present on the most common multitesters available.

67. A: A printed circuit board is an example of a substrate, or underlying support layer, although the non-conductive core is technically the substrate while the imprinted copper is the layer above (and possibly below) it. Varnish and paint would be the opposite of a substrate, being on the surface rather than the lowest or centermost layers of an assembled product. Devices that are located underground may rest upon "substrates" in the geological sense of the word, but even in this context are not the substrates themselves.

68. A: The registration of a patent means that the invention becomes publicly known, and its commercial use may be licensed to interested parties. When an invention is retained as a secret, it is not subject to legal expirations and thus may be used as such indefinitely. Or, the secret to be kept from competitors is that a commonly known technique is being used for a specific purpose. Some forms of processes, such as most recipes for food, cannot be patented at all.

69. C: The vernier compass was invented to distinguish the magnetic pole of the Earth from the center of the Earth's rotation, the latter being considered true north for the purpose of creating and reading maps. The other options are all other kind of surveying instruments: the theodolite measures vertical and horizontal angles; a transit is a special invertible kind of theodolite; and a wye level establishes the flat base angle of the Earth's surface by gravitation, and is held in place by wye rings.

70. D: An industrial standard is a measure of quality or best practice and is typically established by professional organizations or national/state law. Individual manufacturers can and do create standards of their own, but the term industrial standard primarily refers to industry-wide conventions. Consumer protection groups may also create standards, but these are observational rather than the guiding force of the actual work or product being observed. International standards may be adopted, but any legislative mandate is created nationally or by state and local governments.

71. B: A new machine costs $1,000 and lasts ten years before obsolescence, or in other words costs $100 a year. The older machine costs only $50 a year to maintain until reaching

its obsolescence, a cheaper option. Keeping the older machine for ten years is not a viable option, as this would take it beyond the point where it becomes obsolete. Likewise, retaining it for an indeterminate period of time would cause the same problem, and so this is also not the best answer. Based on the information given, the five-year option is less costly, while addressing the issue of obsolescence.

72. A: The term biotechnology in a broad sense can mean primitive and traditional methods of using plant or animal products, but usually refers to certain innovative applications. Of these, the applied science of genetics is by far the most commonplace. As technical literacy requires understanding what is being discussed, an understanding of probable intentions is important. Methods of sealing wood could involve such technology, but this is not specified. Biomechanical designs are a narrow subset of the general term.

73. D: Plotter printers draw lines, while most other printing techniques compose images from series of dots. Raster graphics are an example of dot composition. The terms font and typeface are generic terms for symbols that may be generated by a variety of methods, not only or mainly plotter printers. Vector graphics are composed of solid lines; the term can refer to both types of printing, such as the plotter printer, and to image displays such those as used in monitors known as vectorscopes.

74. C: When a saw begins a cut on the edge of a board, there may be little need for guides to be cut beforehand, although notches are sometimes utilized. However, a cut in the middle of a board needs a space to allow the jigsaw blade access to the full thickness of the board. Additionally, the evenness of the final cut is improved immensely by defining a definite beginning and end. The steps of sanding the board, applying varnish, and attaching accessories are final steps after the primary structure of the piece is done.

75. C: A dust mask is of course intended to stop dust from entering the respiratory system of the user. Therefore the answer to the question involves a dust-producing activity. The application of paints, as well as the chemicals used for tanning leather, often produces vapors that require ventilation; a dust mask is not designed for vapors. Cutting metal may produce sharp flying shards, but a dust mask is not strong enough to be of help. Sanding wood, especially if done by machine, can produce clouds of small particles that cause irritation if inhaled, thus requiring the protection of a dust mask.

76. B: The best option given is the pacing and scheduling of work, as this is usually a business decision. All the other options require greater input technical expertise, although management would make the final decisions in any event. Customer relations are the responsibility of marketing, sales, and similar customer service departments. Deciding on materials requires the input of management to arbitrate on the basis of economic realities and likewise decisions of personnel. However, the managerial input for scheduling is greater than for the other options.

77. A: The interchangeability of identical parts is seen as a hallmark of the modern manufacturing process, from the beginning of the Industrial Revolution through present times. The remaining options are also characteristic of the same modern, assembly line oriented systems. However, they do not specifically address the question, which asks about assembly of parts, rather than design and planning, or what happens after the assembly is complete and the product is used by consumers.

78. A: It is important to avoid discrimination against students and parents from lower socioeconomic backgrounds. This necessitates consideration of access to expensive appliances and services such as the internet or even telephones. While in many situations these are adequate for reaching an entire student population or most individuals in that population, consideration must be given to economically disadvantaged households. The remaining options represent subjective decisions that may be relevant to certain situations.

79. B: While any level of quality could be chosen for video, and any other level for corresponding audio tracks, the most commonly used ratios are usually in the low hundreds. This practice is founded on the concept that video information inherently contains about two hundred times the information of audio, although this of course is to some extent an arbitrary distinction. Thus, the ultimate basis of the ratio rests in large part upon the expectations of the viewers, who may otherwise be expected to find other ratios distracting, or may lead to an impression of low quality.

80. B: Radio transmissions, including those used for television and wireless telephones, are regulated and primarily enforced at the federal level. The application of fume-producing surface treatments is also subject to federal safety regulations, as well as regulation of the disposal of waste products resulting from application. Local ordinances may add to these regulations but are not the primary regulatory means. Combustion-propelled model rockets are often restricted within city limits by ordinances similar to those restricting fireworks.

81. A: All of the options are oft-cited justifications for including humanities courses, such as for literature and history, with engineering-oriented degree plans. However, the remaining options are subsets of the correct answer. The question asks for the best answer, which in this case is the most inclusive answer. A better understanding of client priorities and communication might, for instance, lead to better recognition of environmental priorities, and would most certainly require adequate skills of grammar and spelling.

82. B: Modern technology education is often described as a laboratory rather than a workshop, with a greater emphasis on the underlying science of technology than in the past. However, the theoretical science must pertain to an applied use in a technological context. Of the options given, only the production of video games specifically mentions such an application. The remaining options could be tied into applications, but these are not mentioned. Standardized assessments for students of these courses are uncommon, particularly at the state-sponsored K-12 level.

83. B: Biological catalysts can be harvested from bacterial colonies and other organic sources for the purpose of industrial applications. This represents a major category of use for the innovative modern techniques, often but not exclusively involving genetic engineering, known as biotechnology. In particular, it is an application beyond that of biological systems: the catalysts are not used to directly affect living things or the products of living organisms, which is the subject of the remaining options.

84. A: Many innovative systems for producing mechanical power, such as the propulsion of an automobile, employ hybrids of both petroleum-based fuels and electrical motors, such as a motor powered with electricity generated by an internal combustion engine. However, the energy savings derived from these systems comes from sources such as energy recovered from braking, powering down when the vehicle is idling, and similar devices. No mechanical

- 100 -

device is 100% efficient, so adding more steps means more wasted energy. Diesel engines are generally more energy efficient than gasoline power.

85. D: Total quality control is a term for evaluating how effective a company's standards are. The other options presume that standards have been set, and that sufficient or insufficient performance is derived from these established norms. Company quality examines the human interactions which may affect quality. Failure testing involves the generation of actual data regarding a product, while statistical control takes these results and derives a relevant meaning such as how likely a given product is to fail under conditions of use.

86. C: The task of a marketing department is to find out what customers want and how much they are willing to pay. These parameters are then passed on to other departments such as management and engineering. The engineers must then create designs that reflect those needs and economic realities. All of the options are similar practical considerations, but cost is the best choice because it directly involves evaluating customer requests or needs.

87. A: Of the listed options, the American National Standards Institute deals with the most diverse range of products, including consumer products such as printer paper. The Institute of Electrical and Electronic Engineers, as well as the Institute of Nuclear Materials Management, can be discounted because of the specific industries mentioned in their names. This leaves a choice between the American National Standards Institute and the National Institute of Standards and Technology. Of these two, the name of the latter has a greater connotation of high tech and industrial applications.

88. D: Push-button combination locks are primarily found mounted on doors, rather than simply attached by the locking mechanism itself. Compact electronic keypad locks are available, but expensive and excessive for the stated use. Multiple dial locks are easy to use but are notoriously easy to break, leading to the common choice of self-contained, single dial locks for most student use. Latches of lockers are often made specifically to accommodate this variety of lock.

89. B: The nominal size of lumber refers to boards that have not yet been planed or sanded into the regular rectilinear shapes necessary to fit one board tightly against another. Reference charts made for this purpose assume that a half-inch or three-quarters of an inch will be lost to planing, so woodworkers must plan for such differences. The difference is only relevant to width and depth, not to the length of a board. The length is commonly equal to or a little longer than the stated dimension.

90. B: The oscillations referenced by the term oscilloscope typically mean repeating waves of energy, such as radio signals or similar applications of electricity or light. Literal rotations of mechanical parts may be adjusted by devices such as the strobe lights used to adjust the timing of belts. The finding of surface defects may be addressed by a magnifying glass or microscope, while periscopes are used to see into the recessed and otherwise inaccessible interiors of machines.

91. D: The electrostatic charge functions much like the way dust collects. Static electricity causes dust to cling onto the surfaces of electrical appliances and similarly charged objects, such as carpets or furniture. By intentionally creating such a charge during the painting process, adhesion is improved. Demagnetization would involve an effectively opposite

process. The paints used vary in terms of resolvability. Corrosion resistance is only one of several benefits derived from improved paint adhesion.

92. C: Oxygen is a corrosive, highly reactive element. Often in the manufacturing process, these characteristics are particularly undesirable. However, simply removing the surrounding air would be both costly and would subject materials to stress from the pressure changes required to create a vacuum. Air-like mixtures without oxygen are therefore employed. Barring extraordinary laboratory conditions, argon reacts with nothing. Nitrogen is relatively nonreactive and is cheaper than argon, and so usually constitutes the greater part of these mixtures.

93. B: Fiber optics are most commonly used for communicating data. Other uses do in fact involve magnification, using the optical cable as a kind of periscope to inspect the interiors of machines or even medical uses within a patient's body, but this means that the image conveyed is subject to magnification after leaving the optical cable itself. Textiles and agriculture use other kinds of fibers in various applications, but these generally do not use the optical image transmissions of images or of light patterns.

94. C: While this problem could be solved with mathematical operations, there is an easier method, one which has led to the common use of certain scale ratios. There are 12 inches to a foot, with most rulers dividing an inch into sixteenths. Because 12 times 16 is 192, 1/16th of an inch equals 1 foot in a 1:192 scale. We may thus read sixteenths as feet without any further calculation. The arithmetic for this problem is 3 ? 192 = 576, or 576/16th inches. 576 ? 16 = 36 inches; 36 divided by the 12 inches in a foot equals 3 feet.

95. D: Computer semiconductor chips are composed of thin films over a thin substrate, so even without specific familiarity with the process of chemical vapor deposition, the correct answer may be inferred. Increasingly obsolete methods of motion picture production use film, hence the term films meaning movies, but this is not specifically relevant to the topic of the question. Some methods of finishing furniture and the surfaces of automobiles use film-like substances, not typically in the deposition process mentioned.

96. D: Gear ratios are expressed in consideration of the origin of power, that is, which gear is turning which. The pinion, the often smaller gear which transmits power from an engine or other source, becomes the denominator (if the information is expressed as a fraction). That is, for each revolution of the larger gear mentioned in the problem, the power-conveying pinion gear revolves 1.44 times. The information could theoretically be expressed in opposite terms, yielding a ratio of 0.69:1, but this is not the common convention of usage.

97. B: In analog video, the camera is adjusted to be insensitive to green or blue light, while modern digital video simply removes the designated color from each bit of information. A superimposed picture-within-a-picture is a related technique, but is not specifically mentioned in the question or prompt. Focal length is not directly relevant. The overall effect is to remove green light, not to bathe the subject in green light visible to the viewer.

98. C: Lubrication is the primary function of water when used with sandpaper. Sealing is often undertaken to prevent water from contacting and degrading a surface. The common use of water as a cleaner is not directly relevant, nor is the role of the water jets that are used in mining operations to remove debris from the path of a drill. Some modern forms of

stonecutting use jets of water to produce cuts in a block of stone, but this is not relevant to sandpaper.

99. C: Epoxy adhesives are supplied to the consumer in two parts, an adhesive and a hardener for the adhesive. The two portions react chemically when mixed, forming a single durable compound. Depending on the variety used, some contraction or expansion may occur, but this is generally minimized in order to allow close fitting of parts to be bonded together. Some adhesives must be melted or otherwise softened prior to use, but this is not directly relevant to the question.

100. C: The question refers specifically to improved crops, meaning plants and their edible or otherwise usable produce. Within this classification, the transference of genes is a major technique for altering the plants. The remaining options are peripheral factors that contribute to the quality of crops but do not contribute as closely, or that cannot be considered a part of the plants themselves. Soil treatments affect the plants but are not identical to the plants, while irradiation of the produce occurs after the produce is separated from the living plant.

Secret Key #1 - Time is Your Greatest Enemy

Pace Yourself

Wear a watch. At the beginning of the test, check the time (or start a chronometer on your watch to count the minutes), and check the time after every few questions to make sure you are "on schedule."

If you are forced to speed up, do it efficiently. Usually one or more answer choices can be eliminated without too much difficulty. Above all, don't panic. Don't speed up and just begin guessing at random choices. By pacing yourself, and continually monitoring your progress against your watch, you will always know exactly how far ahead or behind you are with your available time. If you find that you are one minute behind on the test, don't skip one question without spending any time on it, just to catch back up. Take 15 fewer seconds on the next four questions, and after four questions you'll have caught back up. Once you catch back up, you can continue working each problem at your normal pace.

Furthermore, don't dwell on the problems that you were rushed on. If a problem was taking up too much time and you made a hurried guess, it must be difficult. The difficult questions are the ones you are most likely to miss anyway, so it isn't a big loss. It is better to end with more time than you need than to run out of time.

Lastly, sometimes it is beneficial to slow down if you are constantly getting ahead of time. You are always more likely to catch a careless mistake by working more slowly than quickly, and among very high-scoring test takers (those who are likely to have lots of time left over), careless errors affect the score more than mastery of material.

Secret Key #2 - Guessing is not Guesswork

You probably know that guessing is a good idea - unlike other standardized tests, there is no penalty for getting a wrong answer. Even if you have no idea about a question, you still have a 20-25% chance of getting it right.

Most test takers do not understand the impact that proper guessing can have on their score. Unless you score extremely high, guessing will significantly contribute to your final score.

Monkeys Take the Test

What most test takers don't realize is that to insure that 20-25% chance, you have to guess randomly. If you put 20 monkeys in a room to take this test, assuming they answered once per question and behaved themselves, on average they would get 20-25% of the questions correct. Put 20 test takers in the room, and the average will be much lower among guessed questions. Why?

1. The test writers intentionally write deceptive answer choices that "look" right. A test taker has no idea about a question, so picks the "best looking" answer, which is often wrong. The monkey has no idea what looks good and what doesn't, so will consistently be lucky about 20-25% of the time.

2. Test takers will eliminate answer choices from the guessing pool

based on a hunch or intuition. Simple but correct answers often get excluded, leaving a 0% chance of being correct. The monkey has no clue, and often gets lucky with the best choice.

This is why the process of elimination endorsed by most test courses is flawed and detrimental to your performance- test takers don't guess, they make an ignorant stab in the dark that is usually worse than random.

$5 Challenge

Let me introduce one of the most valuable ideas of this course- the $5 challenge:

You only mark your "best guess" if you are willing to bet $5 on it.
You only eliminate choices from guessing if you are willing to bet $5 on it.

Why $5? Five dollars is an amount of money that is small yet not insignificant, and can really add up fast (20 questions could cost you $100). Likewise, each answer choice on one question of the test will have a small impact on your overall score, but it can really add up to a lot of points in the end.

The process of elimination IS valuable. The following shows your chance of guessing it right:

If you eliminate wrong answer choices until only this many remain:	Chance of getting it correct:
1	100%
2	50%
3	33%

However, if you accidentally eliminate the right answer or go on a hunch for an incorrect answer, your chances drop dramatically: to 0%. By guessing among all the answer choices, you are GUARANTEED to have a shot at the right answer.

That's why the $5 test is so valuable- if you give up the advantage and safety of a pure guess, it had better be worth the risk.

What we still haven't covered is how to be sure that whatever guess you make is truly random. Here's the easiest way:

Always pick the first answer choice among those remaining.

Such a technique means that you have decided, **before you see a single test question**, exactly how you are going to guess- and since the order of choices tells you nothing about which one is correct, this guessing technique is perfectly random.

This section is not meant to scare you away from making educated guesses or eliminating choices- you just need to define when a choice is worth eliminating. The $5 test, along with a pre-defined random guessing strategy, is the best way to make sure you reap all of the benefits of guessing.

Secret Key #3 - Practice Smarter, Not Harder

Many test takers delay the test preparation process because they dread the awful amounts of practice time they think necessary to succeed on the test. We have refined an effective method that will take you only a fraction of the time.

There are a number of "obstacles" in your way to succeed. Among these are answering questions, finishing in time, and mastering test-taking strategies. All must be executed on the day of the test at peak performance, or your score will suffer. The test is a mental marathon that has a large impact on your future.

Just like a marathon runner, it is important to work your way up to the full challenge. So first you just worry about questions, and then time, and finally strategy:

Success Strategy

1. Find a good source for practice tests.
2. If you are willing to make a larger time investment, consider using more than one study guide- often the different approaches of multiple authors will help you "get" difficult concepts.
3. Take a practice test with no time constraints, with all study helps "open book." Take your time with questions and focus on applying strategies.
4. Take a practice test with time constraints, with all guides "open book."
5. Take a final practice test with no open material and time limits

If you have time to take more practice tests, just repeat step 5. By gradually exposing yourself to the full rigors of the test environment, you will condition your mind to the stress of test day and maximize your success.

Secret Key #4 - Prepare, Don't Procrastinate

Let me state an obvious fact: if you take the test three times, you will get three different scores. This is due to the way you feel on test day, the level of

preparedness you have, and, despite the test writers' claims to the contrary, some tests WILL be easier for you than others. Since your future depends so much on your score, you should maximize your chances of success. In order to maximize the likelihood of success, you've got to prepare in advance. This means taking practice tests and spending time learning the information and test taking strategies you will need to succeed.

Never take the test as a "practice" test, expecting that you can just take it again if you need to. Feel free to take sample tests on your own, but when you go to take the official test, be prepared, be focused, and do your best the first time!

Secret Key #5 - Test Yourself

Everyone knows that time is money. There is no need to spend too much of your time or too little of your time preparing for the test. You should only spend as much of your precious time preparing as is necessary for you to get the score you need.

Once you have taken a practice test under real conditions of time constraints, then you will know if you are ready for the test or not.

If you have scored extremely high the first time that you take the practice test, then there is not much point in spending countless hours studying. You are already there.

Benchmark your abilities by retaking practice tests and seeing how much you have improved. Once you score high enough to guarantee success, then you are ready.

If you have scored well below where you need, then knuckle down and begin studying in earnest. Check your improvement regularly through the use of practice tests under real conditions. Above all, don't worry, panic, or give up. The key is perseverance!

Then, when you go to take the test, remain confident and remember how well you did on the practice tests. If you can score high enough on a practice test, then you can do the same on the real thing.

General Strategies

The most important thing you can do is to ignore your fears and jump into the test immediately- do not be overwhelmed by any strange-sounding terms. You have to jump into the test like jumping into a pool- all at once is the easiest way.

Make Predictions

As you read and understand the question, try to guess what the answer will be. Remember that several of the answer choices are wrong, and once you begin reading them, your mind will immediately become cluttered with answer choices designed to throw you off. Your mind is typically the most focused immediately after you have read the question and digested its contents. If you can, try to predict what the correct answer will be. You may be surprised at what you can predict.

Quickly scan the choices and see if your prediction is in the listed answer choices. If it is, then you can be quite confident that you have the right answer. It still won't hurt to check the other answer choices, but most of the time, you've got it!

Answer the Question

It may seem obvious to only pick answer choices that answer the question, but the test writers can create some excellent answer choices that are wrong. Don't pick an answer just because it sounds right, or you believe it to be true. It MUST answer the question. Once you've made your selection, always go back and check it against the question and make sure that you didn't misread the question, and the answer choice does answer the question posed.

Benchmark

After you read the first answer choice, decide if you think it sounds correct or not. If it doesn't, move on to the next answer choice. If it does, mentally mark that answer choice. This doesn't mean that you've definitely selected it as your answer choice, it just means that it's the best you've seen thus far. Go ahead and read the next choice. If the next choice is worse than the one you've already selected, keep going to the next answer choice. If the next choice is better than the choice you've already selected, mentally mark the new answer choice as your best guess.

The first answer choice that you select becomes your standard. Every other answer choice must be benchmarked against that standard. That choice is correct until proven otherwise by another answer choice beating it out. Once you've decided that no other answer choice seems as good, do one final check to ensure that your answer choice answers the question posed.

Valid Information

Don't discount any of the information provided in the question. Every piece of information may be necessary to determine the correct answer. None of the information in the question is there to throw you off (while the answer choices will certainly have information to throw you off). If two seemingly unrelated topics are discussed, don't ignore either. You can be confident there is a relationship, or it wouldn't be included in the question, and you are probably going to have to determine what that relationship is to find the answer.

Avoid "Fact Traps"

Don't get distracted by a choice that is factually true. Your search is for the answer that answers the question. Stay focused and don't fall for an answer that is true but incorrect. Always go back to the question and make sure you're choosing an answer that actually answers the question and is not just a true statement. An answer can be factually correct, but it MUST answer the question asked. Additionally, two answers can both be seemingly correct, so be sure to read all of the answer choices, and make sure that you get the one that BEST answers the question.

Milk the Question

Some of the questions may throw you completely off. They might deal with a subject you have not been exposed to, or one that you haven't reviewed in years. While your lack of knowledge about the subject will be a hindrance, the question itself can give you many clues that will help you find the correct answer. Read the question carefully and look for clues. Watch particularly for adjectives and nouns describing difficult terms or words that you don't recognize. Regardless of if you completely understand a word or not, replacing it with a synonym either provided or one you more familiar with may help you to understand what the questions are asking. Rather than wracking your mind about specific detailed information concerning a difficult term or word, try to use mental substitutes that are easier to understand.

The Trap of Familiarity

Don't just choose a word because you recognize it. On difficult questions, you may not recognize a number of words in the answer choices. The test writers don't put "make-believe" words on the test; so don't think that just because you only recognize all the words in one answer choice means that answer choice must be correct. If you only recognize words in one answer choice, then focus on that one. Is it correct? Try your best to determine if it is correct. If it is, that is great, but if it doesn't, eliminate it. Each word and answer choice you eliminate

increases your chances of getting the question correct, even if you then have to guess among the unfamiliar choices.

Eliminate Answers

Eliminate choices as soon as you realize they are wrong. But be careful! Make sure you consider all of the possible answer choices. Just because one appears right, doesn't mean that the next one won't be even better! The test writers will usually put more than one good answer choice for every question, so read all of them. Don't worry if you are stuck between two that seem right. By getting down to just two remaining possible choices, your odds are now 50/50. Rather than wasting too much time, play the odds. You are guessing, but guessing wisely, because you've been able to knock out some of the answer choices that you know are wrong. If you are eliminating choices and realize that the last answer choice you are left with is also obviously wrong, don't panic. Start over and consider each choice again. There may easily be something that you missed the first time and will realize on the second pass.

Tough Questions

If you are stumped on a problem or it appears too hard or too difficult, don't waste time. Move on! Remember though, if you can quickly check for obviously incorrect answer choices, your chances of guessing correctly are greatly improved. Before you completely give up, at least try to knock out a couple of possible answers. Eliminate what you can and then guess at the remaining answer choices before moving on.

Brainstorm

If you get stuck on a difficult question, spend a few seconds quickly brainstorming. Run through the complete list of possible answer choices. Look at each choice and ask yourself, "Could this answer the question satisfactorily?" Go through each answer choice and consider it independently of the other. By systematically going through all possibilities, you may find something that you would otherwise overlook. Remember that when you get stuck, it's important to try to keep moving.

Read Carefully

Understand the problem. Read the question and answer choices carefully. Don't miss the question because you misread the terms. You have plenty of time to read each question thoroughly and make sure you understand what is being asked. Yet a happy medium must be attained, so don't waste too much time. You must read carefully, but efficiently.

Face Value

When in doubt, use common sense. Always accept the situation in the problem at face value. Don't read too much into it. These problems will not require you to make huge leaps of logic. The test writers aren't trying to throw you off with a cheap trick. If you have to go beyond creativity and make a leap of logic in order to have an answer choice answer the question, then you should look at the other answer choices. Don't overcomplicate the problem by creating theoretical relationships or explanations that will warp time or space. These are normal problems rooted in reality. It's just that the applicable relationship or explanation may not be readily apparent and you have to figure things out. Use your common sense to interpret anything that isn't clear.

Prefixes

If you're having trouble with a word in the question or answer choices, try dissecting it. Take advantage of every clue that the word might include. Prefixes and suffixes can be a huge help. Usually they allow you to determine a basic meaning. Pre- means before, post- means after, pro - is positive, de- is negative. From these prefixes and suffixes, you can get an idea of the general meaning of the word and try to put it into context. Beware though of any traps. Just because con is the opposite of pro, doesn't necessarily mean congress is the opposite of progress!

Hedge Phrases

Watch out for critical "hedge" phrases, such as likely, may, can, will often, sometimes, often, almost, mostly, usually, generally, rarely, sometimes. Question writers insert these hedge phrases to cover every possibility. Often an answer choice will be wrong simply because it leaves no room for exception. Avoid answer choices that have definitive words like "exactly," and "always".

Switchback Words

Stay alert for "switchbacks". These are the words and phrases frequently used to alert you to shifts in thought. The most common switchback word is "but". Others include although, however, nevertheless, on the other hand, even though, while, in spite of, despite, regardless of.

New Information

Correct answer choices will rarely have completely new information included. Answer choices typically are straightforward reflections of the material asked about and will directly relate to the question. If a new piece of information is included in an answer choice that doesn't even seem to relate to the topic being asked about, then that answer choice is likely incorrect. All of the information needed to answer the question is usually provided for you, and so you should not have to make guesses that are unsupported or choose answer choices that require unknown information that cannot be reasoned on its own.

Time Management

On technical questions, don't get lost on the technical terms. Don't spend too much time on any one question. If you don't know what a term means, then since you don't have a dictionary, odds are you aren't going to get much further. You should immediately recognize terms as whether or not you know them. If you don't, work with the other clues that you have, the other answer choices and terms provided, but don't waste too much time trying to figure out a difficult term.

Contextual Clues

Look for contextual clues. An answer can be right but not correct. The contextual clues will help you find the answer that is most right and is correct. Understand the context in which a phrase or statement is made. This will help you make important distinctions.

Don't Panic

Panicking will not answer any questions for you. Therefore, it isn't helpful. When you first see the question, if your mind goes blank, take a deep breath. Force yourself to mechanically go through the steps of solving the problem and using the strategies you've learned.

Pace Yourself

Don't get clock fever. It's easy to be overwhelmed when you're looking at a page full of questions, your mind is full of random thoughts and feeling confused, and the clock is ticking down faster than you would like. Calm down and maintain the pace that you have set for yourself. As long as you are on track by monitoring your pace, you are guaranteed to have enough time for yourself. When you get to the last few minutes of the test, it may seem like you won't have enough time left, but if you only have as many

questions as you should have left at that point, then you're right on track!

Answer Selection

The best way to pick an answer choice is to eliminate all of those that are wrong, until only one is left and confirm that is the correct answer. Sometimes though, an answer choice may immediately look right. Be careful! Take a second to make sure that the other choices are not equally obvious. Don't make a hasty mistake. There are only two times that you should stop before checking other answers. First is when you are positive that the answer choice you have selected is correct. Second is when time is almost out and you have to make a quick guess!

Check Your Work

Since you will probably not know every term listed and the answer to every question, it is important that you get credit for the ones that you do know. Don't miss any questions through careless mistakes. If at all possible, try to take a second to look back over your answer selection and make sure you've selected the correct answer choice and haven't made a costly careless mistake (such as marking an answer choice that you didn't mean to mark). This quick double check should more than pay for itself in caught mistakes for the time it costs.

Beware of Directly Quoted Answers

Sometimes an answer choice will repeat word for word a portion of the question or reference section. However, beware of such exact duplication – it may be a trap! More than likely, the correct choice will paraphrase or summarize a point, rather than being exactly the same wording.

Slang

Scientific sounding answers are better than slang ones. An answer choice that begins "To compare the outcomes..." is much more likely to be correct than one that begins "Because some people insisted…"

Extreme Statements

Avoid wild answers that throw out highly controversial ideas that are proclaimed as established fact. An answer choice that states the "process should be used in certain situations, if…" is much more likely to be correct than one that states the "process should be discontinued completely." The first is a calm rational statement and doesn't even make a definitive, uncompromising stance, using a hedge word "if" to provide wiggle room, whereas the second choice is a radical idea and far more extreme.

Answer Choice Families

When you have two or more answer choices that are direct opposites or parallels, one of them is usually the correct answer. For instance, if one answer choice states "x increases" and another answer choice states "x decreases" or "y increases," then those two or three answer choices are very similar in construction and fall into the same family of answer choices. A family of answer choices is when two or three answer choices are very similar in construction, and yet often have a directly opposite meaning. Usually the correct answer choice will be in that family of answer choices. The "odd man out" or answer choice that doesn't seem to fit the parallel construction of the other answer choices is more likely to be incorrect.

Special Report: What is Test Anxiety and How to Overcome It?

The very nature of tests caters to some level of anxiety, nervousness or tension, just as we feel for any important event that occurs in our lives. A little bit of anxiety or nervousness can be a good thing. It helps us with motivation, and makes achievement just that much sweeter. However, too much anxiety can be a problem; especially if it hinders our ability to function and perform.

"Test anxiety," is the term that refers to the emotional reactions that some test-takers experience when faced with a test or exam. Having a fear of testing and exams is based upon a rational fear, since the test-taker's performance can shape the course of an academic career. Nevertheless, experiencing excessive fear of examinations will only interfere with the test-takers ability to perform and his/her chances to be successful.

There are a large variety of causes that can contribute to the development and sensation of test anxiety. These include, but are not limited to lack of performance and worrying about issues surrounding the test.

Lack of Preparation

Lack of preparation can be identified by the following behaviors or situations:

Not scheduling enough time to study, and therefore cramming the night before the test or exam
Managing time poorly, to create the sensation that there is not enough time to do everything
Failing to organize the text information in advance, so that the study material consists of the entire text and not simply the pertinent information
Poor overall studying habits

Worrying, on the other hand, can be related to both the test taker, and many other factors around him/her that will be affected by the results of the test. These include worrying about:

Previous performances on similar exams, or exams in general
How friends and other students are achieving
The negative consequences that will result from a poor grade or failure

There are three primary elements to test anxiety: 1) Physical components, which involve the same typical bodily reactions as those to acute anxiety (to be discussed below), 2) Emotional factors have to do with fear or panic, and. 3) Mental or cognitive issues concerning attention spans and memory abilities.

Physical Signals

There are many different symptoms of test anxiety, and these are not limited to mental and emotional strain. Frequently there are a range of physical signals that will let a test taker know that he/she is suffering from test anxiety. These bodily changes can include the following:
Perspiring
Sweaty palms
Wet, trembling hands
Nausea
Dry mouth
A knot in the stomach
Headache
Faintness
Muscle tension
Aching shoulders, back and neck
Rapid heart beat
Feeling too hot/cold

To recognize the sensation of test anxiety, a test-taker should monitor himself/herself for the following sensations:
- The physical distress symptoms as listed above
- Emotional sensitivity, expressing emotional feelings such as the need to cry or laugh too much, or a sensation of anger or helplessness
- A decreased ability to think, causing the test-taker to blank out or have racing thoughts that are hard to organize or control.

Though most students will feel some level of anxiety when faced with a test or exam, the majority can cope with that anxiety and maintain it at a manageable level. However, those who cannot are faced with a very real and very serious condition, which can and should be controlled for the immeasurable benefit of this sufferer.

Naturally, these sensations lead to negative results for the testing experience. The most common effects of test anxiety have to do with nervousness and mental blocking.

Nervousness

Nervousness can appear in several different levels:
- The test-taker's difficulty, or even inability, to read and understand the questions on the test
- The difficulty or inability to organize thoughts to a coherent form
- The difficulty or inability to recall key words and concepts relating to the testing questions (especially essays)
- The receipt of poor grades on a test, though the test material was well known by the test taker

Conversely, a person may also experience mental blocking, which involves:
- Blanking out on test questions

- Only remembering the correct answers to the questions when the test has already finished.

Fortunately for test anxiety sufferers, beating these feelings, to a large degree, has to do with proper preparation. When a test taker has a feeling of preparedness, then anxiety will be dramatically lessened.

The first step to resolving anxiety issues is to distinguish which of the two types of anxiety are being suffered. If the anxiety is a direct result of a lack of preparation, this should be considered a normal reaction, and the anxiety level (as opposed to the test results) shouldn't be anything to worry about. However, if, when adequately prepared, the test-taker still panics, blanks out, or seems to overreact, this is not a fully rational reaction. While this can be considered normal too, there are many ways to combat and overcome these effects.

Remember that anxiety cannot be entirely eliminated; however, there are ways to minimize it, to make the anxiety easier to manage. Preparation is one of the best ways to minimize test anxiety. Therefore the following techniques are wise in order to best fight off any anxiety that may want to build.

To begin with, try to avoid cramming before a test, whenever it is possible. By trying to memorize an entire term's worth of information in one day, you'll be shocking your system, and not giving yourself a very good chance to absorb the information. This is an easy path to anxiety, so for those who suffer from test anxiety, cramming should not even be considered an option.

Instead of cramming, work throughout the semester to combine all of the material which is presented throughout the semester, and work on it gradually as the course goes by, making sure to master the main concepts first, leaving minor details for a week or so before the test.

To study for the upcoming exam, be sure to pose questions that may be on the examination, to gauge the ability to answer them by integrating the ideas from your texts, notes and lectures, as well as any supplementary readings.

If it is truly impossible to cover all of the information that was covered in that particular term, concentrate on the most important portions, that can be covered very well. Learn these concepts as best as possible, so that when the test comes, a goal can be made to use these concepts as presentations of your knowledge.

In addition to study habits, changes in attitude are critical to beating a struggle with test anxiety. In fact, an improvement of the perspective over the entire test-taking experience can actually help a test taker to enjoy studying and therefore improve the overall experience. Be certain not to overemphasize the significance of the grade - know that the result of the test is neither a reflection of self worth, nor is it a measure of intelligence; one grade will not predict a person's future success.

To improve an overall testing outlook, the following steps should be tried:
1. Keeping in mind that the most reasonable expectation for taking a test is to expect to try to demonstrate as much of what you know as you possibly can.

2. Reminding ourselves that a test is only one test; this is not the only one, and there will be others.
3. The thought of thinking of oneself in an irrational, all-or-nothing term should be avoided at all costs.
4. A reward should be designated for after the test, so there's something to look forward to. Whether it be going to a movie, going out to eat, or simply visiting friends, schedule it in advance, and do it no matter what result is expected on the exam.

Test-takers should also keep in mind that the basics are some of the most important things, even beyond anti-anxiety techniques and studying. Never neglect the basic social, emotional and biological needs, in order to try to absorb information. In order to best achieve, these three factors must be held as just as important as the studying itself.

Study Steps

Remember the following important steps for studying:

Maintain healthy nutrition and exercise habits. Continue both your recreational activities and social pass times. These both contribute to your physical and emotional well being.

Be certain to get a good amount of sleep, especially the night before the test, because when you're overtired you are not able to perform to the best of your best ability.

Keep the studying pace to a moderate level by taking breaks when they are needed, and varying the work whenever possible, to keep the mind fresh instead of getting bored.

When enough studying has been done that all the material that can be learned has been learned, and the test taker is prepared for the test, stop studying and do something relaxing such as listening to music, watching a movie, or taking a warm bubble bath.

There are also many other techniques to minimize the uneasiness or apprehension that is experienced along with test anxiety before, during, or even after the examination. In fact, there are a great deal of things that can be done to stop anxiety from interfering with lifestyle and performance. Again, remember that anxiety will not be eliminated entirely, and it shouldn't be. Otherwise that "up" feeling for exams would not exist, and most of us depend on that sensation to perform better than usual. However, this anxiety has to be at a level that is manageable.

Of course, as we have just discussed, being prepared for the exam is half the battle right away. Attending all classes, finding out what knowledge will be expected on the exam, and knowing the exam schedules are easy steps to lowering anxiety.

Keeping up with work will remove the need to cram, and efficient study habits will eliminate wasted time.

Studying should be done in an ideal location for concentration, so that it is simple to become interested in the material and give it complete attention.

A method such as SQ3R (Survey, Question, Read, Recite, Review) is a wonderful key to follow to make sure that the study habits are as effective as possible, especially in the case of learning from a textbook. Flashcards are great techniques for memorization.

Learning to take good notes will mean that notes will be full of useful information, so that less sifting will need to be done to seek out what is pertinent for studying. Reviewing notes after class and then again on occasion will keep the information fresh in the mind. From notes that have been taken summary sheets and outlines can be made for simpler reviewing.

A study group can also be a very motivational and helpful place to study, as there will be a sharing of ideas, all of the minds can work together, to make sure that everyone understands, and the studying will be made more interesting because it will be a social occasion.

Basically, though, as long as the test-taker remains organized and self confident, with efficient study habits, less time will need to be spent studying, and higher grades will be achieved.

To become self-confident, there are many useful steps. The first of these is "self talk." It has been shown through extensive research, that self-talk for students who suffer from test anxiety, should be well monitored, in order to make sure that it contributes to self confidence as opposed to sinking the student. Frequently the self talk of test-anxious students is negative or self-defeating, thinking that everyone else is smarter and faster, that they always mess up, and that if they don't do well, they'll fail the entire course. It is important to decreasing anxiety that awareness is made of self talk. Try writing any negative self thoughts and then disputing them with a positive statement instead. Begin self-encouragement as though it was a friend speaking. Repeat positive statements to help reprogram the mind to believing in successes instead of failures.

Helpful Techniques

Other extremely helpful techniques include:

- Self-visualization of doing well and reaching goals
- While aiming for an "A" level of understanding, don't try to "overprotect" by setting your expectations lower. This will only convince the mind to stop studying in order to meet the lower expectations.
- Don't make comparisons with the results or habits of other students. These are individual factors, and different things work for different people, causing different results.
- Strive to become an expert in learning what works well, and what can be done in order to improve. Consider collecting this data in a journal.
- Create rewards for after studying instead of doing things before studying that will only turn into avoidance behaviors.
- Make a practice of relaxing - by using methods such as progressive relaxation, self-hypnosis, guided imagery, etc - in order to make relaxation an automatic sensation.

- Work on creating a state of relaxed concentration so that concentrating will take on the focus of the mind, so that none will be wasted on worrying.
- Take good care of the physical self by eating well and getting enough sleep.
- Plan time for exercise and stick to this plan.

Beyond these techniques, there are other methods to be used before, during and after the test that will help the test-taker perform well in addition to overcoming anxiety.

Before the exam comes the academic preparation. This involves establishing a study schedule and beginning at least one week before the actual date of the test. By doing this, the anxiety of not having enough time to study for the test will automatically be eliminated. Moreover, this will make the studying a much more effective experience, ensuring that the learning will be an easier process. This relieves much undue pressure on the test-taker.

Summary sheets, note cards, and flash cards with the main concepts and examples of these main concepts should be prepared in advance of the actual studying time. A topic should never be eliminated from this process. By omitting a topic because it isn't expected to be on the test is only setting up the test-taker for anxiety should it actually appear on the exam. Utilize the course syllabus for laying out the topics that should be studied. Carefully go over the notes that were made in class, paying special attention to any of the issues that the professor took special care to emphasize while lecturing in class. In the textbooks, use the chapter review, or if possible, the chapter tests, to begin your review.

It may even be possible to ask the instructor what information will be covered on the exam, or what the format of the exam will be (for example, multiple choice, essay, free form, true-false). Additionally, see if it is possible to find out how many questions will be on the test. If a review sheet or sample test has been offered by the professor, make good use of it, above anything else, for the preparation for the test. Another great resource for getting to know the examination is reviewing tests from previous semesters. Use these tests to review, and aim to achieve a 100% score on each of the possible topics. With a few exceptions, the goal that you set for yourself is the highest one that you will reach.

Take all of the questions that were assigned as homework, and rework them to any other possible course material. The more problems reworked, the more skill and confidence will form as a result. When forming the solution to a problem, write out each of the steps. Don't simply do head work. By doing as many steps on paper as possible, much clarification and therefore confidence will be formed. Do this with as many homework problems as possible, before checking the answers. By checking the answer after each problem, reinforcement will exist, that will not be on the exam. Study situations should be as exam-like as possible, to prime the test-taker's system for the experience. By waiting to check the answers at the end, a psychological advantage will be formed, to decrease the stress factor.

Another fantastic reason for not cramming is the avoidance of confusion in concepts, especially when it comes to mathematics. 8-10 hours of study will become one hundred percent more effective if it is spread out over a week or at least several days, instead of doing it all in one sitting. Recognize that the human brain requires time in order to assimilate new material, so frequent breaks and a span of study time over several days will be much more beneficial.

Additionally, don't study right up until the point of the exam. Studying should stop a minimum of one hour before the exam begins. This allows the brain to rest and put things in their proper order. This will also provide the time to become as relaxed as possible when going into the examination room. The test-taker will also have time to eat well and eat sensibly. Know that the brain needs food as much as the rest of the body. With enough food and enough sleep, as well as a relaxed attitude, the body and the mind are primed for success.

Avoid any anxious classmates who are talking about the exam. These students only spread anxiety, and are not worth sharing the anxious sentimentalities.

Before the test also involves creating a positive attitude, so mental preparation should also be a point of concentration. There are many keys to creating a positive attitude. Should fears become rushing in, make a visualization of taking the exam, doing well, and seeing an A written on the paper. Write out a list of affirmations that will bring a feeling of confidence, such as "I am doing well in my English class," "I studied well and know my material," "I enjoy this class." Even if the affirmations aren't believed at first, it sends a positive message to the subconscious which will result in an alteration of the overall belief system, which is the system that creates reality.

If a sensation of panic begins, work with the fear and imagine the very worst! Work through the entire scenario of not passing the test, failing the entire course, and dropping out of school, followed by not getting a job, and pushing a shopping cart through the dark alley where you'll live. This will place things into perspective! Then, practice deep breathing and create a visualization of the opposite situation - achieving an "A" on the exam, passing the entire course, receiving the degree at a graduation ceremony.

On the day of the test, there are many things to be done to ensure the best results, as well as the calmest outlook. The following stages are suggested in order to maximize test-taking potential:
Begin the examination day with a moderate breakfast, and avoid any coffee or beverages with caffeine if the test taker is prone to jitters. Even people who are used to managing caffeine can feel jittery or light-headed when it is taken on a test day.

Attempt to do something that is relaxing before the examination begins. As last minute cramming clouds the mastering of overall concepts, it is better to use this time to create a calming outlook.

Be certain to arrive at the test location well in advance, in order to provide time to select a location that is away from doors, windows and other distractions, as well as giving enough time to relax before the test begins.

Keep away from anxiety generating classmates who will upset the sensation of stability and relaxation that is being attempted before the exam.

Should the waiting period before the exam begins cause anxiety, create a self-distraction by reading a light magazine or something else that is relaxing and simple.

During the exam itself, read the entire exam from beginning to end, and find out how much time should be allotted to each individual problem. Once writing the exam, should more

- 119 -

time be taken for a problem, it should be abandoned, in order to begin another problem. If there is time at the end, the unfinished problem can always be returned to and completed.

Read the instructions very carefully - twice - so that unpleasant surprises won't follow during or after the exam has ended.

When writing the exam, pretend that the situation is actually simply the completion of homework within a library, or at home. This will assist in forming a relaxed atmosphere, and will allow the brain extra focus for the complex thinking function.

Begin the exam with all of the questions with which the most confidence is felt. This will build the confidence level regarding the entire exam and will begin a quality momentum. This will also create encouragement for trying the problems where uncertainty resides.

Going with the "gut instinct" is always the way to go when solving a problem. Second guessing should be avoided at all costs. Have confidence in the ability to do well.

For essay questions, create an outline in advance that will keep the mind organized and make certain that all of the points are remembered. For multiple choice, read every answer, even if the correct one has been spotted - a better one may exist.

Continue at a pace that is reasonable and not rushed, in order to be able to work carefully. Provide enough time to go over the answers at the end, to check for small errors that can be corrected.

Should a feeling of panic begin, breathe deeply, and think of the feeling of the body releasing sand through its pores. Visualize a calm, peaceful place, and include all of the sights, sounds and sensations of this image. Continue the deep breathing, and take a few minutes to continue this with closed eyes. When all is well again, return to the test.
If a "blanking" occurs for a certain question, skip it and move on to the next question. There will be time to return to the other question later. Get everything done that can be done, first, to guarantee all the grades that can be compiled, and to build all of the confidence possible. Then return to the weaker questions to build the marks from there.

Remember, one's own reality can be created, so as long as the belief is there, success will follow. And remember: anxiety can happen later, right now, there's an exam to be written!

After the examination is complete, whether there is a feeling for a good grade or a bad grade, don't dwell on the exam, and be certain to follow through on the reward that was promised...and enjoy it! Don't dwell on any mistakes that have been made, as there is nothing that can be done at this point anyway.

Additionally, don't begin to study for the next test right away. Do something relaxing for a while, and let the mind relax and prepare itself to begin absorbing information again.

From the results of the exam - both the grade and the entire experience, be certain to learn from what has gone on. Perfect studying habits and work some more on confidence in order to make the next examination experience even better than the last one.

Learn to avoid places where openings occurred for laziness, procrastination and day dreaming.

Use the time between this exam and the next one to learn to relax better (even learning to relax on cue), so that any anxiety can be controlled during the next exam. Learn how to relax the body. Slouch in your chair if that helps. Tighten and then relax all of the different muscle groups, one group at a time, beginning with the feet and then working all the way up to the neck and face. This will ultimately relax the muscles more than they were to begin with. Learn how to breathe deeply and comfortably, and focus on this breathing going in and out as a relaxing thought. With every exhale, repeat the word "relax."

As common as test anxiety is, it is very possible to overcome it. Make yourself one of the test-takers who overcome this frustrating hindrance.

Special Report: Retaking the Test: What Are Your Chances at Improving Your Score?

After going through the experience of taking a major test, many test takers feel that once is enough. The test usually comes during a period of transition in the test taker's life, and taking the test is only one of a series of important events. With so many distractions and conflicting recommendations, it may be difficult for a test taker to rationally determine whether or not he should retake the test after viewing his scores.

The importance of the test usually only adds to the burden of the retake decision. However, don't be swayed by emotion. There a few simple questions that you can ask yourself to guide you as you try to determine whether a retake would improve your score:

1. What went wrong? Why wasn't your score what you expected?

Can you point to a single factor or problem that you feel caused the low score? Were you sick on test day? Was there an emotional upheaval in your life that caused a distraction? Were you late for the test or not able to use the full time allotment? If you can point to any of these specific, individual problems, then a retake should definitely be considered.

2. Is there enough time to improve?

Many problems that may show up in your score report may take a lot of time for improvement. A deficiency in a particular math skill may require weeks or months of tutoring and studying to improve. If you have enough time to improve an identified weakness, then a retake should definitely be considered.

3. How will additional scores be used? Will a score average, highest score, or most recent score be used?

Different test scores may be handled completely differently. If you've taken the test multiple times, sometimes your highest score is used, sometimes your average score is computed and used, and sometimes your most recent score is used. Make sure you understand what method will be used to evaluate your scores, and use that to help you determine whether a retake should be considered.

4. Are my practice tests scores significantly higher than my actual test score?

If you have taken a lot of practice tests and are consistently scoring at a much higher level than your actual test score, then you should consider a retake. However, if you've taken five practice tests and only one of your scores was higher than your actual test score, or if your practice tests scores was only slightly higher than your actual test score, then it is unlikely that you will significantly increase your score.

5. Do I need perfect scores or will I be able to live with this score? Will this score still allow me to follow my dreams?

What kind of score is acceptable to you? Is your current score "good enough?" Do you have to have a certain score in order to pursue the future of your dreams? If you won't be happy with your current score, and there's no way that you could live with it, then you should consider a retake. However, don't get your hopes up. If you are looking for significant improvement, that may or may not be possible. But if you won't be happy otherwise, it is at least worth the effort.

Remember that there are other considerations. To achieve your dream, it is likely that your grades may also be taken into account. A great test score is usually not the only thing necessary to succeed. Make sure that you aren't overemphasizing the importance of a high test score.

Furthermore, a retake does not always result in a higher score. Some test takers will score lower on a retake, rather than higher. One study shows that one-fourth of test takers will achieve a significant improvement in test score, while one-sixth of test takers will actually show a decrease. While this shows that most test takers will improve, the majority will only improve their scores a little and a retake may not be worth the test taker's effort.

Finally, if a test is taken only once and is considered in the added context of good grades on the part of a test taker, the person reviewing the grades and scores may be tempted to assume that the test taker just had a bad day while taking the test, and may discount the low test score in favor of the high grades. But if the test is retaken and the scores are approximately the same, then the validity of the low scores are only confirmed. Therefore, a retake could actually hurt a test taker by definitely bracketing a test taker's score ability to a limited range.

Special Report: Additional Bonus Material

Due to our efforts to try to keep this book to a manageable length, we've created a link that will give you access to all of your additional bonus material.

Please visit http://www.mometrix.com/bonus948/texesteched to access the information.